Getting it Right in Print
Digital Prepress for Graphic Designers

Mark Gatter

Harry N. Abrams, Inc., Publishers

Design: Mark Gatter
Cover design: Michael Walsh

Libary of Congress Cataloging-in-Publication Data

Gatter, Mark.
    Getting it right in print : digital prepress for graphic
designers / by Mark Gatter.
            p. cm.
    Includes bibliographical references and index.
    ISBN 0-8109-9206-X (alk. paper)
1. Desktop publishing. 2. Graphic design (Typography) 3. Image processing—Digital
techniques. 4. Printing —Data processing. I. Title.

    Z253.53.G38 2005
    686.2'2—dc22

2004026971

This book was designed and produced by
Laurence King Publishing Ltd, London

Printed and bound in Singapore

10 9 8 7 6 5 4 3 2 1

Harry N. Abrams, Inc.
100 Fifth Avenue
New York, N.Y. 10011
www.abramsbooks.com

Abrams is a subsidiary of

LA MARTINIÈRE
GROUPE

Contents

Acknowledgements

Almost everything I have learned about offset printing and graphic design has come to me through the kindness and patience of many fine and generous people. I would therefore like to take this opportunity to thank the following individuals:

Barry Adalian and Barry Viney for being the world's best mentors.
Alan Raingley and Jack Butterworth for taking a chance and giving me my first job in commercial offset printing.
Vin Smith for being himself, and also for being the finest printer I've ever met.
Robina Courtin for being in a class all of her own in her pursuit of perfection in all things.
Angus Berry for his ability to make light of absolutely everything.
Ron Mullein and Martin Gallagher for their unique approach to graphic design.
Phil and Grace Sharples, Ed Cain, Jean Stubenrauch, Mark Taylor, Charles Gropman, Eve Kline, Carla Winkler, Sheila Burns and Mark Kroninger for being the best print team I've ever had the pleasure of working with.
Cindy Frank and John Fremont for letting me design so many of their book covers.
Nick Ribush for being almost as picky as I am.
Peter Bone for his assistance with some of the more esoteric software questions.
Douglas and Naomi Bellworthy for giving me the opportunity to test-drive so much of this book.
Brian Gerrett and his pre-press team at Friary Press, Dorchester, for continuously pushing the cutting edge of new technology.

I would also like to thank Jo Lightfoot at Laurence King Publishing for her faith in this project, and my editor Nell Webb for the good humor and great patience she managed to maintain while wading through endless piles of information about printing and graphic design.

In addition, I would like to thank my family, in general and specifically: my father for introducing me to the world of typography and printing; my mother for refusing to believe that a leaf changes color in the dark; my brother for thinking up the "leaf test" in the first place; my sister for being a fellow graphic designer; and my dear wife Linda for her incredible support through good times and bad, and for suggesting that I write this book.

—Mark Gatter

Preface

For the past twenty years or so, I have worked extensively in the commercial printing industry and also as a graphic designer, both in the US and in England. I am constantly running into other graphic designers who have degrees or similarly extensive training behind them, but who nevertheless have little or no idea about the actual requirements of the printing process. As a result, every time they send a job to their printer, they experience nail-biting anxiety because they don't know exactly how it's going to turn out.

The specific grey areas that cause this anxiety are things like dot-gain, image calibration, trapping, questions relating to the use of CMYK vs. RGB, and generating error-free PDF documents for the printer.

This book explains all these misunderstood areas, and more, in a way that provides an overview of the entire process, from error-free digital creation right through to commercial printing, and includes detailed instructions that will enable anyone, even complete beginners, to do the necessary work for themselves *before* the job is sent to the print shop.

As well as writing books on the subject, I teach intensive one- and two-day training courses, covering all skill levels from complete beginner up, in the following applications:

Adobe Photoshop	Adobe Illustrator
Adobe PageMaker	Adobe InDesign
QuarkXPress	Macromedia Freehand
CorelDraw	

I also teach two-day digital repro and pre-press courses specifically aimed at graphic designers, and offer private consultation and troubleshooting on questions relating to graphics, printing and print production.

If you would like to know more, please visit my website (www.markgatter.co.uk) or e-mail me (info@markgatter.co.uk).

CHAPTER 1

The Evolution of an Industry

The changing face of graphic design

For many years, the printing industry has been divided into two separate areas of expertise. On the one hand there are those who run the presses and take care of "finishing," i.e cutting, folding, binding, and so on. On the other hand, there are those who supply the jobs to be printed: the graphic designers. Since the early 1980s the work of graphic designers has evolved from the mechanical assembly of the basic layout, into which the printer's photographic department placed the relevant images, to the production of digital files that contain absolutely everything needed for the job.

Digitization has been a major development. Yet, while the methods used to produce digital files continue to evolve at high speed, as each successive version of the various software applications is released, the designer and the printer have generally remained within their own traditionally defined areas of expertise. As a result, many of the physical requirements of the printing process are not understood by the very people who need to understand them most of all, i.e. the graphic designers.

In the early days of digital production, this lack of understanding usually meant that graphic designers went through a period of intense anxiety while they waited to see how their work actually looked in print. Colors might have changed, pictures might look miserable compared to how they appeared on screen, and previously unseen mistakes might suddenly make themselves known.

Rather than improving over time, these problems took a serious turn for the worse in the early 2000s. Printers started to request that jobs be submitted to print shops as a **PDF** (**portable document format**) file rather than in the "native" software in which they were originally put together. While this has made life easier for printers, PDF files are hard—often impossible—to edit. Printers are often unable to fix errors that have been unwittingly included, and the nature of PDF files means that these errors are much harder to see in the first place, leaving responsibility for all of them squarely on the shoulders of the unfortunate designer.

Precise image **calibration**, **dot gain**, **RGB** vs. **CMYK**, screen clash, and

trapping are some of the typical gray areas encountered by graphic designers in digital pre-press today. Such seemingly complex processes are actually not very difficult to deal with, but because they are hardly ever taught, they are often not understood, leading to all sorts of problems on the press that are both expensive and time-consuming to fix.

Graphic designers who can understand and manage these areas with confidence will save time and money on everything they do. In addition, they will no longer find themselves waking up in a panic at 3 A.M., mentally going through their entire production process again and again, looking for possible errors.

How it all started

The printing industry has evolved over many centuries to get to where it is today. Yet far from progressing as a steady stream of innovation, printing continued for hundreds of years without noticeably changing at all. During the past fifty years, however, its acceleration has been phenomenal.

Originally, the complete image of a page was carved onto a piece of wood. In some parts of the world this is still done today. The remaining surface area—the letters—got inked and the cut-out areas did not. When a sheet of paper (or parchment, or vellum) was pressed down onto it and then peeled carefully away, the ink transferred to it and an image was produced. Two of the tricky things regarding this method were 1) what happened if there was a typo (typographical error) and 2) typos were more likely to occur because the page had to be carved as a reversed image of what was actually wanted, which is obviously much harder.

The invention of moveable type was therefore a huge leap forward. Finally, typos could be fixed quickly and easily and, once finished, it could all be taken apart and used again for the next job.

Moveable type was first developed in China in 1041 using not metal but clay characters. It took nearly another 400 years for Johannes Gutenberg to take the next step in Europe and produce the first moveable metal-type printing press in 1440, culminating in the production of the famous Gutenberg Bible in 1455. Unfortunately for him, that was the same year in which his sponsors withdrew their funding, effectively bankrupting him. Illustrations were combined with type for the first time when Albrecht Pfister printed *Edelstein*, which featured a number of woodcuts, in 1461. Fifteen years later, in 1476, William Caxton started printing in England—using typefaces that were intended to look like monk's handwriting—and by the end of that century printing was happening in 250 European cities. However, early in the seventeenth century the realization of the power of the printed word brought strong opposition from both Parliament and the Church. Things became really serious in 1637, when an act was passed limiting the number of printers in England by decree. Then, in 1644, the Licensing Act required all printed material to be approved by an official censor. With penalties that included fines, imprisonment, confiscation of equipment, and even death, this attempt to preserve the existing power structure was alarmingly successful. As a result, by the end of the century there were only twenty master printers in England, eighteen of whom were working in London. Given this kind of obstacle-ridden start, it is amazing that printing survived. However, like the pen, the printed page has proved over time to be mightier than the sword. No wonder freedom of speech and freedom of the press are taken so seriously today.

From letterpress to litho

For centuries, the only kind of commercial printing available was **letterpress**, a process in which a matrix of assembled metal type characters was first inked and then pressed against a sheet of paper, thus transferring the image. Then, in the early 1830s, photography was invented. This paved the way for all kinds of changes, including new methods for creating the images used in letterpress printing and, somewhat later, in **offset litho**. It took about 60 years for offset litho, first used in the early days of the twentieth century, to steal the bulk of the printing market away from letterpress—a market that was still being substantially fought over into the early 1960s. Even in the late 1970s it was by no means uncommon to find a letterpress printer working in the corner of what was otherwise an offset-litho shop.

How did this revolution take place? Initially, through the production of images rather than type. Printers wanted to get away from purely illustrative woodcuts and engravings in favour of realism. But, as with woodcuts and engravings, the problem was how to create all those shades of gray when using just one color of ink: i.e. black. They already knew that it could be done by relying on an optical illusion. Small, thin lines in a woodcut image printed to look like a light gray, while thicker lines looked darker. Finally, in 1890, after several years of experimentation, the American Frederick Ives came up with a method which allowed the whole process to become photographic. He engraved a grid of fine horizontal and vertical lines on a sheet of glass. The image was projected through the glass onto the emulsion-coated side of a sheet of unexposed

film. Since the image could not pass through the engraved lines, it was instead bounced between them, and so what reached the film was not a continuous-tone image (i.e. all the shades of gray between black and white) but spots of light of varying sizes. The result was called a **halftone**. A dark area on the original image would eventually produce a large dot of black ink, and a light part would produce a small dot (fig. **1.1**). Before the image actually made it all the way to the paper, however, there were several other stages to the process.

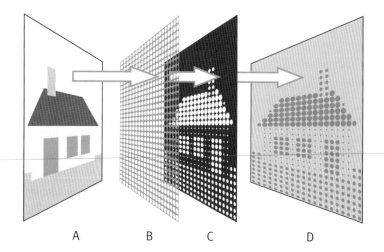

A   B   C   D

1.1

Generating a halftone from a continuous tone image.

Initially, film images were used to make exposures onto **plates** of zinc or copper that were coated with a light-sensitive emulsion. These were then etched and mounted onto blocks of wood—usually oak or mahogany—for use in letterpress printing in exactly the same way that woodcuts and engravings had been. The surface of the block—the image—would get inked, but the background, having been etched away, would not.

Creating a halftone image on either a letterpress block or an offset-litho plate (fig. 1.6) depends on much the same process. Light reflected from the original image (A) travels through a screen (B) and produces halftone dots of varying sizes on a sheet of film (C). This example shows negative film, which has clear dots on a black background. Using positive film would instead give a black dot on a clear background. The image on the film is transferred to the plate (D) through making a "contact" exposure during which the two elements are held firmly together.

In order to make halftone dots clearer and more consistent, the printing industry had to figure out a new kind of film. The emulsion it used was not required to create shades of gray, because that would produce fuzzy-edged dots—and dots in a halftone need to be crisp and clear. If the edges were fuzzy, nobody could say how big the resulting dot was going to be. That is why printing materials such as film and plates work in a sort of binary fashion—on or off. Either there is a clear dot on the film, or there is not; either there is a resulting ink-holding dot on the plate, or there is not; either there is a resulting dot printed on the paper, or there is not. There are, literally, no gray areas. This is because in order to produce a shade of gray, it is necessary to use either gray ink or the white of the paper showing through between all the black dots and thus creating an illusion of gray when seen from a distance. It is all the art of illusion. Fortunately, graphic designers only need to be convincing, and that is a very important thing to remember. In a printed image, if you are close enough to see the dots, you (almost completely) stop seeing the image—and the illusion is therefore not convincing (fig. **1.2**). However, when you cannot see the dots anymore (either because they are too small or too far away) you can only see the (quite convincing) image. Pure

1.2

On the left, we see the dots more than the image.

On the right, we see the image more than the dots.

illusion. Our job is to maintain the illusion as far as possible. (Incidentally, litho film is also completely insensitive to red light, which means that a darkroom technician can run around in the darkroom while there is film lying about, without bumping into everything.)

Advances in typesetting

Despite this great leap forward in the production of photographic images, offset litho, while gaining in popularity, had to continue to wait in the wings until the second half of the twentieth century, when new technology was developed for the production of type. The individual metal and wood letters of letterpress were quite quickly pushed to the side by the much faster and cleaner IBM Selectric (the "golfball" print head typewriter), rub-down type from Letraset (and others), and early **phototypesetting** machines.

Phototypesetting was invented in 1949 but did not really get going until the 1960s. These were darkroom-operated mechanical devices which projected the image of the letters, one at a time, onto a strip of photographic paper. Letterspacing was manually controlled until the advent of automatic spacing in systems like the Monotype Studio Lettering Machine in the early 1970s, a typesetter that was also versatile enough to be able to set type ranging in height from $\frac{1}{8}$ in (3 mm) to 5 in (128 mm).

Computers finally got involved as several manufacturers developed typesetting hybrids that were partly digital and partly mechanical. Type was set using a computer keyboard and a single-color **cathode ray tube (CRT)** screen and coded in the same kind of way as **HTML**. If you wanted the next line of type to be bold, you had to first type the code that said "be bold," then the line of text, and then the code that said "stop being bold." **Linotype** and **Compugraphic** machines contained a wheel on which four strips of film were clamped, each carrying the entire character set of a particular font—which does not mean, for example, the entire Helvetica family; Helvetica Bold is a font, Helvetica Bold Italic is another. The wheel turned at high speed, and as the appropriate letter passed in front of a strobe light, the light fired. The beam passed through the letter, then through one of five lenses mounted on a rotating turret, then through a prism which projected it up onto a roll of photographic paper. At the end of the job, the paper would be advanced into a light-fast container so that it could be removed and transferred to a film processor. The result was a **galley** of type, sometimes several yards long.

Now, of course, computers have taken over completely—not only for the production of type, but in the creation and editing of images, too. But that is not to say that the printer's darkroom is a thing of the past. As mentioned already, things change slowly in printing. Cutting-edge developments of today might still take several decades to become widespread enough for us to take them for granted. Despite recent advances, especially in the area of **computer to plate (CTP)** printing, there are still thousands of print shops all over the world that use their darkrooms on a daily basis. The use of film is still "normal." It is also interesting to note how, in only the last few years, we have gone from a situation in which "whoever has the most fonts, wins" to "whoever has the most fonts... simply has the most fonts." In the days of the Linotype and Compugraphic phototypesetters, a single font film strip cost around $165. Having an extensive font library back then was a very serious matter. Now, however, there are websites from which anyone can download fonts for free. However, beware the "zillion fonts for a buck" collections, which can contain not only fonts of very poor quality but some which may even wreck your whole system.

The font wars

Early computer fonts were **bitmapped**, i.e. the letters displayed at a single, fixed resolution. This meant that a separate font file was required for every different type size needed in a job. **PostScript** "Type 1" fonts, developed by Adobe, were based on **vector** outlines for each character. As vectors are not resolution-dependent, the lettering in a single font could therefore be scaled to whatever sizes were required. PostScript fonts are made up of two files: one to produce a screen image (the "printer font metrics" or "pfm" file) and the other (the "printer font binary" or "pfb" file) to send the vector outline information to the printer. A huge boost for this format came in 1985 when Apple adopted Adobe's PostScript "page description language" (PDL) for the Apple LaserWriter printer. So, first we can see Apple and Adobe benefiting from helping each other out: Adobe by coming up with the PostScript format in the first place, and Apple for adopting it as the format of choice.

Unfortunately, PostScript fonts are not cross-platform compatible, so there was still room for improvement. Not surprisingly, bitmapped fonts could not compete against the advantages of scaleability and soon vanished forever.

Apple, Microsoft and (later) IBM all realized that, unless there were new developments in type, Adobe's monopoly would continue forever. Apple was the first of the three to come up with a solution in the form of "TrueType." Apple traded its new technology with Microsoft in exchange for the latter's TrueImage PostScript clone technology—despite the fact that it was bug-ridden at the time. So, this second major development saw a partnership between Microsoft and Apple.

TrueType characters are also scaleable vector outlines, but they differ from PostScript in that the fonts are made up of a single digital file.

Typographical purists will notice that PostScript characters have a slightly cleaner outline than their TrueType equivalents, but this of course only becomes apparent when they are printed large enough to see each individual outline in great detail. For most work, either will do.

Originally it could sometimes cause problems if a designer used both PostScript and TrueType fonts in the same file. While these early problems were quickly overcome, it is still the case that you should avoid having both TrueType and Type 1 fonts with exactly the same name installed on the same system, whether it is a PC or a Mac.

"Multiple Master" (MM) font format is an extension of the PostScript Type 1 format. Basically it allows a designer to select two different weights of the same typeface and combine them into a single font at any weight between the two. MM fonts require the use of Adobe Type Manager software, but this is close to being a necessity for PostScript fonts anyway.

The next serious advance in type, "OpenType" fonts, has seen a partnership between Adobe and Microsoft who, as part of their agreement, have licensed TrueType and PostScript font technologies to each other. OpenType fonts are unique in that the same file will operate on both PC and Mac systems. Previously, sending a job from a PC to a Mac **imagesetter** either required **PostScripting** first, so that the font information was embedded in the PostScript code that the imagesetter understood, or that the font used on the PC was also installed on the Mac. Even then, reflow of text has been a common and serious problem. As well as being cross-platform compatible, OpenType fonts have the ability to support widely expanded character sets and layout features. They use a single font file for all of the outline, metric and bitmap data, and while all the major graphics applications can make use of OpenType Fonts, users of Adobe InDesign can also access OpenType layout features that will automatically substitute alternate **glyphs** such as automatic **ligatures**, small capitals, **swashes** and old-style figures.

Commercial offset lithography, the printing method with which this book is mostly involved, relies on an image that has been photographically generated on a plate. Plates are typically thin sheets of aluminium coated with a photo-reactive emulsion. When an exposed plate is developed, the image areas tend to attract oil-based inks, whereas the background areas tend to attract water. By keeping a delicate balance between the ink and the water—which is provided by a unit called the damper system—the right stuff sticks to the right areas

Film technology

and what you end up with is something capable of generating a printed image. Although the materials may vary—for example, you can even get paper plates—the basic idea has remained the same. (There is a more detailed discussion of the offset-litho process in chapter 2.)

For an example of how litho film is used to generate a plate, let us assume that we have assembled the art for the entire printed image and taken an accurate photograph of it. This photograph might have been film generated by an imagesetter that got its information from a disk, or it might have been film generated by the paste-up, darkroom and "film stripping" (highly skilled assembly of film from different sources to make up a complete job) departments in a more traditional print shop. In order to make a plate, we have to lay the film, emulsion side down, onto the plate (which is emulsion side up), and expose them both to light in order to transfer the image from one to the other. This is done in a glass-topped vacuum frame which sucks all the air from between film and plate prior to the exposure to ensure a nice, crisp transfer of image. Specks of dust or other foreign bodies trapped inside create intense pinpoints of uneven pressure which show up on the glass as **Newton's Rings** (fig. **1.3**). These are dark, rainbow-colored concentric circles that show where subsequent problems might occur. Obviously enough, if a foreign object

1.3
Newton's Rings.

gets caught between the film and the plate in the middle of a halftone, there will be a distortion of the resulting plate image at that point. So the operator scans the whole plate area carefully for any sign of Newton's Rings. If they show up in a potentially dangerous area, the operator turns off the vacuum, waits for the pressure to equalize, then lifts the lid to remove the speck. Sometimes it takes a while to make a good plate. When it finally looks clean, the operator can start the exposure, which is usually done with ultraviolet light. This cooks the surface emulsion and hardens it, so that when the plate is developed, the image is left behind while the background is washed away.

There are some geographical differences in the process, depending on where in the world you happen to be. In the US, negative-working film and plates are much more common, whereas in Europe and the Far East almost everyone uses positive-working materials instead. Either way, it does not make too much difference. Negative plates can (usually) be protected for future use with a thin coating of gum arabic, whereas the image on positive plates will (usually) continue to be affected by light and will not be of much use to anyone shortly after the protective layer of ink has been washed off. Negative plates will (usually) need to be replaced part of the way through very long runs, whereas positive plates can (usually) keep on going well beyond 100,000 impressions. There are, of course, exceptions to all these generalizations, but to detail the differences between the most common materials in use worldwide would require a great deal of space, and as it is information that is mostly useful only to a printer trying to match the appropriate materials to a specific job, it is information that is not of much use to a designer. The suitability of that match, however, can be part of the reason why the quote from one print shop might be very different from the quote from another. A good price depends on the availability of the appropriate press and the most cost-effective materials, given the size of the printed piece and the number of copies required.

Film and plate processors are now to be found everywhere, and their use avoids most of the difficulties inherent in manual plate and film developing. Chemicals circulate so that they are maintained at a constant strength, the temperature is held at the optimum level, and working materials are pulled through on rollers ensuring that they are only kept in the various solutions—traditionally a sequence of developer, fixative and wash—for the correct length of time. Plate processors especially are to be found in shops running CTP and **direct imaging (DI)** operations, which do not bother with film at all.

Computer to plate (CTP)

CTP technology has been with us for roughly a decade at the time of writing. However, the spread of new technology in the world of printing

Film*less* technology

has always been slow and sure rather than quick and upsetting, and film-bound offset-litho methods are still by far the most common. There are obvious advantages to the new technology, however, and we are sure to see the traditional methods becoming progressively less common as time goes by. Even so, as printing presses tend not to wear out very quickly, we can expect the transition to continue to be slow.

In a CTP workflow, digital files are used to make plates instead of generating film as a first stage. Because there is no film, image faults caused by foreign objects getting between the film and plate, as well as the expensive and time-wasting revisions they can cause, are a thing of the past. There are also no **registration** problems caused by "film stretch." The degradation of dots caused by **dot gain** (see chapter 7) is diminished, because one of the stages at which the image is physically (rather than digitally) transferred from one medium to another has been removed from the process. Printed images are therefore sharper and registration is better. Environmentally there are benefits, too, because there is no longer a need for the chemicals associated with film processing.

Direct imaging (DI)

Direct imaging takes CTP a step further. Not only is film cut out of the process, the plates themselves are imaged right on the press by an array of lasers. The images thus generated hold ink in just the same way as on conventional offset litho machines. This means that everything required for the job arrives on-press perfectly positioned—i.e. registered—with no further positioning adjustments required, therefore saving considerable time in getting the job ready to roll. As the main advantage of DI over other methods is this decrease in set-up time, it tends to attract short-run work requiring a fast turnaround.

The best thing about CTP technology is that by removing film from the process, quality is (potentially) increased, and cost and turnaround time are reduced. The best thing about DI technology is that it removes yet another step and sends digital data directly to the press. The next big question, therefore, is whether DI printing will kill off the CTP market in the same way that CTP is (gradually) killing off the film market. Again, expect any transition to be slow. CTP is a technology that can be used with conventional presses, and these will continue to have a place on the shop floor for many years to come.

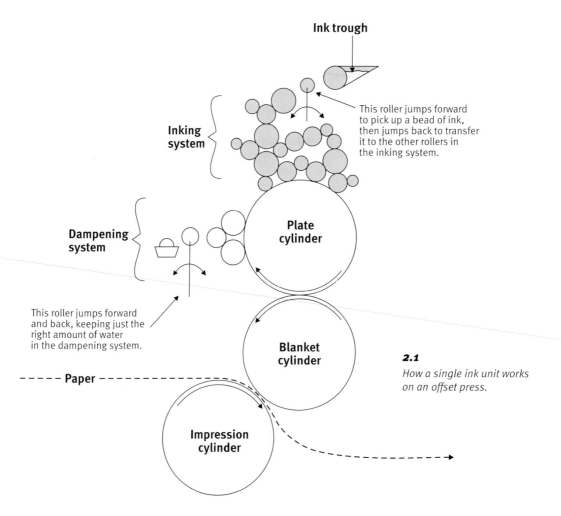

Ink trough

Inking system

This roller jumps forward to pick up a bead of ink, then jumps back to transfer it to the other rollers in the inking system.

Dampening system

Plate cylinder

This roller jumps forward and back, keeping just the right amount of water in the dampening system.

Blanket cylinder

Paper

2.1

How a single ink unit works on an offset press.

Impression cylinder

("offset") to the blanket cylinder, a roller covered with a canvas-backed sheet of rubber. Hence the term "offset printing."

The blanket, being rubber, can press down hard on the paper with no problem. Simultaneously, the impression cylinder is pressing up from underneath. The resulting pressure keeps the paper from slipping as it moves between the two, thus creating a sharp image.

After the last unit on the press, the paper hits a stop bar just as the grippers let go of it and settles onto an ever-increasing pile on another trolley. Typically, **sheet-fed presses** are run at around 3,000 sheets an hour (fig. **2.2**).

Paper is very heavy stuff. It is made mostly from wood pulp, and a stack of it sitting on a pressroom trolley can easily weigh 450 lb or more. After the first run through the press, the side facing down is nice clean paper— but the other side, facing up, is fresh, wet ink.

2.2

The front end of an 8-color Heidelberg press, running at full speed.

So why is it that the clean side of a sheet does not stick to the wet side of the sheet underneath it? That is also a kind of "offset," by the way, but in this instance it is called **set-off**.

The answer is quite simple: cornstarch.

Printers call it "offset spray"—perhaps "cornstarch" would not sound "printerly" enough—but it is the same stuff. The idea is that, just as the grippers let go and the sheet starts to fall gently onto the stack, an air blower puffs out a little cloud of offset spray beneath it—just enough to ensure a few particles, and therefore a very small space, is left between each sheet. Offset spray used in this way is too fine to see, but when a stack is dry you can sometimes feel it as a slight roughness on the paper surface.

Since it tends to build up around the end of the press, the printer will occasionally use compressed air to blast it all away—thus creating a

automated systems in use which are able to provide much faster and more consistent results.

Gravure

Gravure (or Rotogravure) is the printing method that makes banknotes so hard to forge. It uses either a diamond-etched copper plate or a laser-etched polymer resin plate, but either way the actual process is the same.

Gravure plates are very thick compared to those of sheet-fed and web offset. Instead of the ink adhering to the portions of the plate that are left as a raised surface, gravure plates rely on using a much thinner ink that fills the "cells" etched into it. The deeper the cell, the more ink is held—and the darker the corresponding dot on the paper. Excess ink is continually wiped off the raised surfaces of the revolving plate by a steel blade.

Because the ink is thinner, it spreads when it hits the page. This means that the printed result appears to be continuous tone, making gravure the highest-quality option for image reproduction—but conversely a lower-quality option for type, which will also be made up of the same kind of cells as the image.

Originally, gravure cells were all of equal size but varying depths, but now it is possible to use cells of varying size as well. Gravure plate-making is extremely expensive, and as it is also a web-printing process it is much more involved (and therefore more expensive) to set up and run than a simple sheet-fed press. As a result, gravure is usually only suited to extremely long press runs.

An environmental note...

Printing—whichever method you choose—is a messy business. Aside from that, it is usually a highly toxic one. Film chemicals are nasty, as is the developer used on plates; the inks contain all sorts of heavy metals and the solvents used to remove them afterwards are usually varying grades of jet aircraft fuel. If you can, please encourage your printer to use a more environmentally friendly system. There are water-developing plates and soy-based inks available, and if you use a computer-to-plate system film can be cut out of the process altogether. Of course, you should always try to use recycled paper whenever possible. (A single weekend edition of the *New York Times* requires the wood from more than fifty acres of forest.)

Do not assume that the kind of paper you want is not made in a recycled stock—the range available today is huge. Just call your printers and talk to them.

CHAPTER 3

A Word about Paper

Paper weights and sizes

Not only are the US and the UK two nations separated by a common language, they also use different paper sizes and calculate paper "weight" (which usually, but not always, indicates thickness) differently. As well as having thickness and size, paper also has a grain. It is similar to the grain in wood, and is caused by the tendency of the individual paper fibres to line up along the length of the manufactured roll rather than across it. All these are factors to consider when choosing the stock you want.

In the US, paper is of three basic groups: text (also called "book") papers, cover stocks, and a group combining "bond," "writing," and "ledger" paper. Sizes for all these are measured in inches, and weights are calculated in terms of how many pounds (lbs) 500 sheets (one "ream") of the "parent" size stock weigh. For text and book papers, the weight is calculated on a ream of parent sheets measuring 25 x 38 in. Cover stocks are based on a parent size of 20 x 26 in, writing papers on 17 x 22 in, and bond and ledger sheets on 19 x 24 in. In addition to those, there is also a range of card stocks—the kind of thing used for postcards, for example—that are not measured in terms of weight but in terms of thickness. A typical postcard might be described as 10-point C1S ("C1S" translates as "coated one side"), meaning not that it is as thick as a 10 pt type character but that its thickness is $^{10}/_{1000}$ of an inch.

The standard letter size in the US is $8\frac{1}{2}$ x 11 in.

Many other standard sizes are available in addition to, but based on, the parent size. For example, a text sheet might be described as an 80 lb stock measuring 19 x 25 in. Cover stock, which is of course usually heavier, might be given as 60 lb and measure 20 x 26 in. In both these instances, the second dimension also indicates the **grain direction**. Therefore a 19 x 25 in sheet cannot actually be cut from one measuring 25 x 38 in, but it could be cut from one measuring 38 x 25 in.

In the UK, the commonest sizes of sheet are based on one called "A0," which covers a total of one square metre and measures $33\frac{1}{8}$ x $46\frac{3}{4}$ in (841 x 1189 mm). This can be cut in half along the long edge to produce an A1 sheet, which is 33 $\frac{1}{8}$ x 23 $\frac{3}{8}$ in (841 x 594 mm). This can be cut in half in the same way to produce an A2, 16 $\frac{1}{2}$ x 23 $\frac{3}{8}$ in (420 x 594 mm), and so on. An A4, the standard letter-sized sheet, measures 8 $\frac{1}{4}$ in (210 mm) wide x 11 $\frac{3}{4}$ in (297 mm) tall.

Sheet thickness is based on the weight of a 1-metre square; therefore, an A4 page could be 90 gsm (grams per square metre) or 130 gsm, which would be correspondingly thicker.

Sometimes paper is deliberately made fluffier in order to give it added opacity, as in the case of many paperback books. In this case, its weight might be the same as a similar sheet that has been compressed further, but its thickness would be greater.

Of course, printers usually need to print on something larger than an A4 page in order to end up giving you an A4 page. Unless there is extra dimension, there is nowhere for registration marks, printer's marks (blocks of varying tints used to measure ink density), or trim marks. So there are two additional size standards, based on the "A" series, which include a set amount of "trim," the area into which those things useful to a printer can be placed. The smaller of the two adds "R" to the page-size formula (for instance, an RA4 measures 8 $\frac{1}{4}$ x 12 in/215 x 305 mm), and allows for a very small trim. The larger of the two is the "SR" series (as in SRA4, measuring 8 $\frac{3}{4}$ x 12 $\frac{5}{8}$ in/225 x 320 mm), which gives the printer a bit more space to allow for more information. The SR series is generally easier for printers to work with, and enables them to produce a higher-quality end product.

There are two other standard sheet sizes in the UK, the "B" and "C" series. A B0 sheet measures 39 $\frac{3}{8}$ x 55 $\frac{5}{8}$ in (1000 x 1414 mm), and is halved to produce a B1 of 39 $\frac{3}{8}$ x 27 $\frac{7}{8}$ in (1000 x 707 mm) and so forth. A C0 sheet is 36 $\frac{1}{8}$ x 51 in (917 x 1297 mm) and halves to give a C1 of 36 $\frac{1}{8}$ x 25 $\frac{1}{2}$ in (917 x 648 mm), etc. Note that when halving the long edge dimension of any of these standard sizes produces an odd half millimetre, it is rounded down to the next full number.

Envelopes can be a real pain everywhere. Although there are many different standard sizes, the likelihood of finding the particular size you want in the particular stock you want sometimes feels like an impossible dream. Even if you do find it, the chances are there will not be enough in stock to fill your order. If you are designing a job that also requires an envelope, think ahead and prepare to be flexible. Paper availability is not something that improves over time, and over the past several years it has been steadily going from bad to worse. As you will invariably be asking your printer to order stock for you, it is generally better to check up on envelope availability—and paper, too, if you intend to choose anything other than something fairly run-of-the-mill—and then design the job around stock that you know is available.

In order to produce your work, the printer will invariably need to purchase sheets of one of the standard sizes. This may be cut down for the press, or used straight out of the package. If you specify an odd page size, it may mean that there is much more "spoilage"—i.e. a higher proportion of the page will have to be cut off and discarded—than if you had used something closer to a standard. In this case, therefore, you should not only expect a higher paper cost, you should be aware that you might be asking the printer to work harder than normal—something none of us usually appreciates. Non-standard sizes and orientations can mean a more difficult job for the folder, for example; this means more of the sheets will be damaged, therefore more will need to be ordered in the first place. Also, as paper always folds more easily with the grain rather than against it, heavier stocks that also require folding will either be ordered so that the grain goes with the fold, or an additional score will be added.

Imposition

If you are only interested in printing single images such as posters, **imposition** will not affect you. But any time you are printing a multiple-page piece it becomes very important. Imposition is the name given to the configuration in which the pages are positioned on the larger press-sheet, enabling the job to run cost-effectively through the printer, folder and binder.

If you know the basic rules of imposition, you will be able to configure your work to be more efficient. For example, each side of a sheet of paper counts as a page. Therefore a single sheet would be a 2-page insert in a book—but there is no way to include a single sheet other than by physically glueing it into place close to the spine, or making it slightly wider than a regular page so that it can be bound-in, leaving a narrow and unsightly tab adjacent to the binding. Either way, it is an undesirable result.

In order to avoid this situation, multiple-page jobs should always be calculated to generate a page count which is a multiple of 4, or 8, or (best of all if it is possible) 16. As each **signature** (i.e. each separate sheet which, when printed and folded, will be bound together as a book/magazine/newsletter) requires individual handling, if you can end up with two 16-page signatures it is a more efficient way of producing a book than ending up with one 16-page, one 8-page, and one 4-page signature, even though the latter has a smaller total page count. With two 16-page signatures, the folder only has to be set up once to deal with the whole job. With the latter scenario, three separate set-ups are required on the folder and three pick-ups instead of two are needed to collect the signatures together for binding. Of course, that does not mean you should just stick with two 16-page signatures even though it will mean four blank pages at the end of the book. It just means that you have to bear in mind what is best for the job.

The way the pages are positioned within the configuration of a single signature depends on the size of the press, which limits the number of pages it is possible to place on a single plate, the total number of pages in the publication and the way in which it is being bound. For an example, let us take an 8-page newsletter and a plate size which can handle all eight pages together. It will then be folded and **saddle-stitched**, i.e. stapled along the fold, and trimmed on three sides. To see how the pages will need to be imposed, take a single sheet of paper. Fold it in half, and it becomes a 4-page signature. Fold it in half again, and it is an 8-page signature. Take a pen and number the loose corners (and in only one of the four corners of the folded sheet will there be eight loose corners) from 1 to 8. When you unfold the page, the result should look like fig. **3.1**. Side one will carry numbers 1, 8, 4 and 5; side two will have numbers 2, 7, 6 and 3. Incidentally, this is called a **folding dummy**, and is a very useful thing to include with the **laser proofs** you send to the printer.

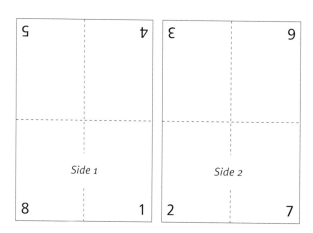

3.1
Both sides of an unfolded 8-page signature, showing page numbering.

The way the printer would want to set this up is called a **work-and-turn** format in which side one of a 4-page section occupies the left-hand half of the plate, and side two occupies the right hand half. The press sheet is then printed, picking up both images. Then it is "turned" over (fig. **3.2**) and run through again. The result is two complete 8-page signatures, one on each half of the press sheet.

3.2

An 8-page signature set up on a plate as a "work-and-turn." The shaded area along the top of the sheet indicates the "gripper edge."

Additional space for a trim has been added above and below the horizontal fold across the center of the sheet. This allows the fold to be trimmed off eventually without affecting the intended page size.

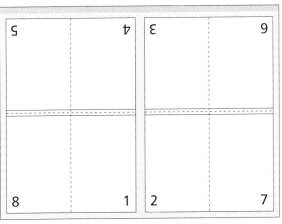

One of the advantages of using the work-and-turn format is that the press can grab the sheet along the same gripper edge for both print runs. This means that the image on one side can be registered to the image on the reverse very accurately, even if the paper has been cut slightly out of square at the mill, as is often the case. If the press sheets are printed using a **work-and-tumble** format, in which the sheets are turned over along the short edge instead, the gripper edge changes. This can make it much more difficult—or even impossible—to properly register both sides of the job to each other. Therefore, the paper for a work-and-tumble press run is usually "cut square" beforehand, i.e. trimmed slightly to ensure that each corner is exactly 90 degrees.

An instance of a job requiring a work-and-tumble press run is given in fig. **3.3**. This shows both sides of a 10-panel brochure, with the panels positioned so that when the sheets are "tumbled," the five reverse panels will "back up" the five panels on the front side, again producing two brochures from each press sheet. Of the two configurations, printers definitely prefer to use work-and-turn.

There is a third possible printing configuration called **sheetwise**. In a sheetwise run, separate plates are needed to print both sides of the sheet.

This could be because only one side of the job can fit on the plate (for example, a large poster) or because the requirements of one side of the sheet will not allow for a work-and-turn or a work-and-tumble format—as in a postcard run, for instance, where four colors will be printed on one side of the sheet but only one color on the reverse.

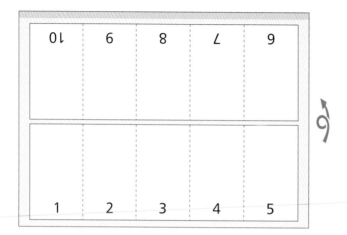

3.3
A work-and-tumble press sheet. Typically a work-and-tumble will only be used for jobs which are impossible to print as a work-and-turn, as in this case—a 10-panel brochure.

Binding can affect imposition placement, depending on whether the signatures will be collected one inside the other and then saddle-stitched, as for a magazine, or collected side by side and then sewn or glued together, as for a hardcover or paperback book. As each successive signature is gathered for saddle-stitching, the thickness of the paper builds up along the binding and pushes those signatures towards the center of the publication further and further out (fig. **3.4**). This is known as **creep**, and can be adjusted for as part of the imposition process. Signatures gathered side-by-side do not create the same kind of build-up, so the problem does not arise.

3.4
Saddle-stitched publications are prone to "creep:" displacement caused by a build-up of paper along the binding.

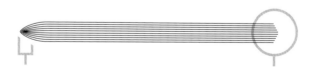

A build-up of paper here...   ...causes the "creep" effect here.

Four-Color Printing Explained

C M Y ...K?

Most graphic designers know that the inks used in four-color process printing are cyan, magenta, yellow and black (CMYK). While it is reasonable to abbreviate cyan, magenta and yellow to C, M, and Y, how come black is given the letter K? Here is how I found out...

Towards the end of my very first day working in the printing industry, one of the printers told me that he needed a new "key plate" first thing the next morning. I had no idea what he meant and thought he was joking. When I eventually arrived an hour after him the following day, he was not happy, to say the least.

This was not good. When the presses stop, the shop is no longer printing money. A new key plate, I was rapidly informed, is a plate that prints the color that all the other colors key to: i.e. black. If you think about it, it is obvious. Text and image borders are typically printed in black. Printing them first often makes it easier to position—or "key"—the other colors to the job. So "key" is actually what the "K" stands for.

It is a common misconception that black is assigned the letter "K" because if it was called "B" it could be confused with blue. While plausible, this is not the case.

Screen angles and screen clash

As we have already seen (see chapter 1), if you want to print a photograph using black ink, you used to have to break it up into dots by bouncing the image through a screen and onto film. Now, of course, you can use software like Adobe Photoshop and desktop scanners instead, but it is the same idea. Your scanner and computer can do a great job of capturing the image, and the imagesetter—the machine that outputs film from your files—**rasterizes** the result, i.e. turns all the **pixel** information into halftone dots. Whichever method you use, screen or software, the end result is an illusion of an image that is actually made up of a grid of dots arranged in long lines at 90 degrees to each other.

This is why at a print shop they do not talk about dots so much as about the lines of dots that together make up a screen of dots. It is not a 150-dot halftone; it is a 150 "line screen" halftone. Different press technologies and papers can only handle certain densities of screen, so the decision as to which one you use is important. But more of that later.

Printing the first color is no problem. But what happens when you want to print an image in more than one color? That means you are planning to print two screens of dots, one on top of the other. The results can be quite a surprise:

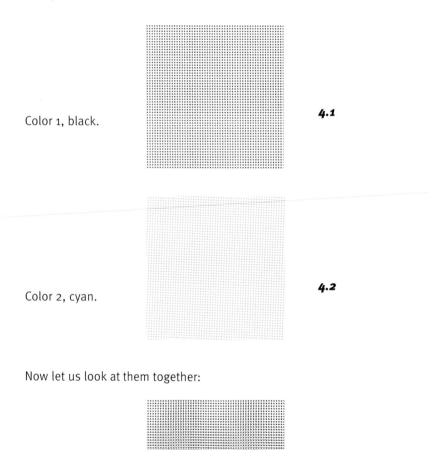

Color 1, black.

4.1

Color 2, cyan.

4.2

Now let us look at them together:

4.3
A moiré pattern.

This unfortunate result (fig. **4.3**) is called a moiré pattern. It is caused when two screens are laid down at close to the same angle and clash. Every few lines, the dots collide. However, printers discovered that if the second screen is turned until the rows of dots are 30° away from the first, the problem goes away (see fig. **4.4**).

4.4
*The two colors together
but at non-conflicting
screen angles.*

So, color 1 can appear with a screen angle of 0° and 90°—i.e. the rows of dots are arranged on a grid of horizontal and vertical lines. Color 2 is turned 30° away from it. Color 3 has to be turned 30° away from both of them. So far, this is what you have (fig. **4.5**):

4.5
*Three of the CMYK components
separated by 30° increments.*

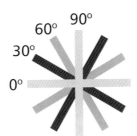

Given that the colors need to be separated by 30° spaces, where can you put color number 4? There is simply nowhere for it to go. If you rotate it another 30°, you are back to where you started—on 0° and 90°. Fortunately, the answer lies in the nature of the colors themselves.

Consider the way we see colors. Obviously enough, we see black as the darkest, yellow as the lightest and cyan and magenta fall somewhere in between. When any one of them is printed as a fine screen (around 150 lines to the inch), the dots are so small we cannot see them even if we hold the sheet only 10–12 in (250–300 mm) away from us. Yellow is even harder to distinguish. It is so invisible to us as a shape that we have not even noticed it causing a moiré pattern in every four-color print we have ever seen. And yet that is exactly what it does. Yellow can slide in between any two of the other colors, only 15° away from both of them. It always causes a moiré, and we never, ever see it. But this is not the case with any of the other colors.

Printers take things even further. As well as there being a range of relative visibility in the colors themselves, there are more- and less-visible screen angles. Not surprisingly, the most visible orientations—the ones which we will see more easily than any of the others—are 0° and 90°. When you think about it, it makes perfect sense. Our world is filled with vertical and horizontal objects, and so we are especially used to noticing those particular angles.

The least-visible orientation is 45°, and this is where black, the most visible color, is placed.

Remember, all this is simply intended to maintain the illusion. That is all you need to do.

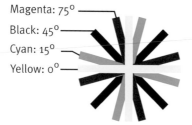

Magenta: 75°
Black: 45°
Cyan: 15°
Yellow: 0°

4.6
The four CMYK components shown at the correct screen angles for printing.

To recap, yellow, the least visible color, goes in at 0° (or 90°), the most visible angle.

Black, the most visible color, goes in at 45°, the least visible angle.

Magenta and cyan are placed 30° either side of black, one at 15° and the other at 75°—and it does not matter which of them goes where (fig. **4.6**).

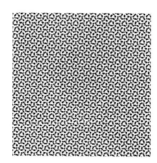

4.7
All four CMYK colors, each printed as a screen at the correct angle.

When these print as a screen of dots, and each color is set at the correct angle, there is no visible moiré pattern at all (fig. **4.7**). And that is the secret of the four-color process.

Beyond four colors

There are two likely contenders for the title of "the next great leap forward" in the evolution of this technology. One is in the use of **stochastic**, or **frequency-modulated**, screens. As already mentioned, in a conventional halftone the dots are locked into a grid pattern. Therefore, in order to display (the illusion of) different shades of a color, they have to vary in size. However, on an inkjet printer all the dots are the same size. In order for them to convey the same illusion, they absolutely cannot be locked into a grid. Instead, they are sprayed out in an apparently random fashion at varying densities. Because there are no grids to cause screen clash, the image is no longer subject to moiré patterns, and because of that, any number of additional colors can be added to extend the range well beyond that of conventional CMYK inks.

Disadvantages of the process are mostly in dealing with the extremely small dots needed to create a convincing image. If the dots are too big, the result looks grainy—even though the dots are actually much smaller than those in a conventional halftone. If the dots are too small, even a tiny amount of dot gain can wipe them out altogether, or make them repeatedly plug up on the press.

Some imagesetters can now produce "hexachrome" (i.e. six-color) separations using stochastic screens of around 600 **dpi** (dots per inch, actually meaning pixels per inch, the accepted measurement of image resolution), good enough for a high-quality print. In hexachrome separations, orange and green are added to the CMYK range in order to extend those areas that are most difficult to duplicate conventionally.

The other "next step" also uses hexachrome separations but in a different way. The two additional colors, orange and green, are the opposites of cyan and magenta, respectively (see chapter 5 for a detailed discussion of color opposites). Therefore, any given color will contain only one of the pair—orange or cyan; green or magenta—but not both. Therefore both colors in each pair can occupy the same screen angle, because they never actually occupy the same space within the image. Thus they do not create a moiré pattern, making it possible to use conventional halftone screening with a six-color hexachrome process instead of CMYK's four.

Pantone Inc. is pioneering the development of this system, and claims that over 90 percent of its **Pantone Matching System** color range can be matched using hexachrome inks (see chapter 15). Therefore, the range of color possible extends far beyond conventional CMYK inks and will allow graphic designers to get much closer in print to colors that, so far, they have only been able to work with on-screen.

Another advantage to printers using this system is that, instead of continuously washing one custom-mixed ink after another off the press, they will be able to stay with the six hexachrome colors for almost everything they want to print. Because of this, the packaging industry—which tends to use a lot of custom color mixes—has pioneered customer use of this new technology.

CHAPTER 5

Understanding Color

RGB VS. CMYK

The main reason I decided to write this book is because so many of my students have had the same, miserable experience of sending their files to the printer and getting back something that is radically different in color from what they were expecting. They know something is seriously wrong, but they have no idea what it is—and therefore cannot fix it.

This chapter discusses what is wrong, and how to begin fixing it. To start with, let us have a closer look at RGB and CMYK.

Firstly, what does RGB mean? R is red, G is green, B is blue. You probably knew that already, but would you know how to get yellow using RGB? It is actually extremely difficult to think in terms of RGB, and yet that is the method your computer uses to display every single color. RGB is the format that scanners and digital cameras use, too. So, all the images you see on your computer actually start out in RGB format, regardless of what is done to them afterwards. There is just no getting away from it.

However, we have already seen in the last chapter how the CMYK colors work, so surely that is the most important format to know about when sending files off for printing. If that is the case, do you really need to bother about RGB? The answer is yes, because unless you know what to avoid, and how to avoid it, RGB will be getting in your way forever, and you will never be able to feel confident about whether you are going to end up getting the printed colors you want.

It will not work merely to change everything into CMYK as soon as it is on-screen—even though, of course, it is essential that everything you eventually send to the printer is in CMYK format (unless it is a multi-channel "extension" of CMYK which also contains spot-color information—see the **"DCS"** section of chapter 11). So, while the change to CMYK does need to be made, it is that change, and the way in which it occurs, that usually cause the problems.

The first thing we need to understand is that RGB refers to different colors of light, whereas CMYK refers to different colors of pigment. We have all developed some level of understanding about the way pigments mix together since someone first gave us a paintbrush and a box of paints. If there is a color we need but do not have, we probably already have a pretty good idea of how we might create it using the "primary" colors. These are colors that cannot themselves be mixed, but from which we can mix a whole lot of "secondary" colors. For instance, if we want green—a secondary color—we would mix together the primary colors blue and yellow. For purple, we would mix blue and red. For orange, yellow and red, and so on.

All the paints we have ever used share this kind of characteristic, and CMYK is just a particularly limited range of paints: we only get four colors, and everything else we need has to be mixed from them.

RGB is, in a way, even more limited because there are only three colors in the palette. Yet these colors mix in such a different way that it is possible to get a much wider range of colors out of them than with CMYK. Unfortunately, many graphic designers have absolutely no idea at all about what the result will be when they mix them, because nobody ever gave them a paintbox containing colors made of light.

As well as being fundamentally different color systems, there is another big problem with CMYK versus RGB. RGB is *almost* the exact opposite of CMYK, but not quite, and that is the cause of many color-related problems for the graphic designer. By the end of this chapter I hope you will understand what I mean by "almost exact opposites."

CMYK and RGB are different in other ways, too.

- Because they are made of light, RGB colors can be seen in the dark. CMYK colors, being made up of pigments, cannot.
- CMYK is called a "subtractive" system because the C, M, and Y components in theory combine to absorb all light and produce black. Of course, in practice, they do not. RGB is called an "additive" system, because it does (almost) the opposite.

Can you trust your monitor?

If you have ever had the experience of having an image that looks a certain way on-screen, but then prints to look radically different, your lack of control over the change from RGB to CMYK is extremely likely to be the reason. However, it may not be the only reason.

When you convert an image from RGB to CMYK mode, your monitor has no choice but to display the new CMYK version using RGB colors. So, an additional problem is that, as far as final, printed color is concerned, *your monitor cannot be trusted.*

Incidentally, there is a very small range of colors within the CMYK range that you cannot produce with RGB. Pure cyan is one of them. So is pure yellow. But do not worry. Strangely enough, even though these are two of the primary CMYK colors, it is very unlikely to be a problem. Problems are much more likely to be caused by being unable to create an RGB color using CMYK rather than the other way around.

Color opposites

Taking a quick look at how color photography works is a good way to start getting a better understanding of the differences between RGB and CMYK.

When we take a picture, the colors coming in through the lens are made up of light, not pigment. So, the input information (light) is obviously much closer to RGB format than it is to CMYK. However, the light hits the film and causes the chemical emulsions on its surface to react. Those chemicals result in colors that are much closer to the pigments used in CMYK than they are to those found in RGB. When the film is developed (print film, not slides), what we actually have on it is a color negative of the image that came in through the lens.

If we examine a film negative we will see that when we take a picture of something magenta, the resulting image on the film negative is green. If we photograph something orange, the resulting image is blue. If it was light in color, the resulting image on the film is dark. Every part of the image on the film is the opposite of the elements in the scene we actually photographed.

Then, to get a positive print, an exposure is made through the image onto photographic print paper. White light is projected through the film and becomes tinted by all the colors in the negative image. If it goes through a green area, the light which travels through to the photographic paper beneath it has picked up a green tint, which then develops to give us the opposite—a magenta area. And so on. The end result is usually a very convincing picture of whatever we were pointing the camera at when we took the shot.

So, even in a camera, the colors created by light and those created by pigments act as opposites. By using their understanding of this fundamental difference, photographers and printers have been able to develop some incredibly sophisticated methods in order to get the exact results they want.

The same kind of understanding can be used by the designer in order to get the desired results in print.

39

Early developers of the CMYK system had to work with the opposites of RGB because pigments of red, green and blue are a hopelessly inadequate palette by themselves. It is impossible to mix them to create anything close to the range of colors required to print a photographic image. But their opposites work very well.

Cyan is as close as we can get, in pigment form, to the opposite of the red in RGB. Magenta is as close as we can get to the opposite of RGB green. Yellow is closest to the opposite of RGB blue. But none of them are exact opposites.

If you wanted to create white with CMYK, you would simply leave them all out. If you wanted to do the same thing using RGB, you would include them all at 100%. In that example, RGB and CMYK act as exact opposites of each other. But what happens when we try to create black?

It seems obvious, at least for the CMYK part of the equation: do not bother with the C, M, or Y, but use plenty of K.

The thing is, if the two systems were exact opposites we would be able to get black using just C, M, and Y. But we cannot, and that is why black had to be added as a fourth color—because you simply cannot create it with C, M, and Y.

So, by their natures, the two systems are exact opposites when it comes to creating white, but they are not exact opposites when it comes to creating black. That is what I mean when I say they are "almost exact" opposites. To sum up:

Question: How do we get black using RGB?
Answer: We turn them all off (in other words, we turn off the lights).
Question: How do we get black using C, M, and Y?
Answer: It is not possible. The combination of the three, even at full strength, is not dark enough to be convincing. That is why we have to include black.

Actually, it is debatable whether we can even get black with black.

When I was in art school, a friend announced that his forthcoming masterpiece was to be a huge canvas painted black. The result, far from being a laughing matter, was quite a shock. The canvas was indeed painted black—but had first been divided into big squares, and each square then filled with a different "black" medium. Oil paint, water paint, poster paint, ink...all the usual "black" pigments were there—but also boot polish, stove paint, soot and even a black plastic sheet.

Looking at the finished work, all the "blacks" appeared to have a particular color tint. The black plastic was obviously blue; the soot, in comparison, looked slightly red. And so on. This was a major revelation for me: color is relative, and you cannot see black when you still have the lights on. (Even with the lights off you would not really see black. Your eyes will not let you, only flickerings here and there.)

To take another example, try looking at something that is black. The only reason you can see it is because it is reflecting light into your eyes. That is the basis of your visual image. And if it is reflecting light, if you can see definition and shading, then you cannot be seeing something which is perfectly black—because true black could only appear in the total absence of light. It is an absence of reflection, definition and shading. In other words, black is a very profound state of "lights off".

When it comes to printing, you have to use something as close to true black as possible because, as previously mentioned, you cannot create anything really close to it with just cyan, magenta and yellow. The pigment used is usually carbon, which makes black the cheapest of all the ink colors. And of course, while it is not really black, that is what we all call it. While its inclusion is essential, a typical four-color separation will contain less black than it will of the other three colors. Black tends to be found around clearly defined edges—it is what helps define them—and of course you will find it in the deep shadows. But there probably will not be very much of it anywhere else. On the other hand, cyan, magenta and yellow will usually be present at higher densities throughout the entire tonal range of the image.

Aside from the need for it in images, black is obviously useful for other things as well—type, for example.

Now that we have some idea how the two systems compare, let us try to create yellow with both of them. Incidentally, in the formula shown in fig. **5.1** the "K" is in parentheses because it is only included to enable the CMYK range to extend to "black" and dark colors close to it. As yellow is the lightest color in the range, K will not be needed at all.

I mentioned earlier that (CMYK) cyan and (RGB) red are more-or-less opposites, as are (CMYK) magenta and (RGB) green, as are (CMYK) yellow and (RGB) blue.

Handily enough, the combination of (RGB) red and (RGB) green is also the opposite of (RGB) blue. Similarly, the combination of (CMYK) cyan and (CMYK) magenta is the opposite of (CMYK) yellow. So, in order to get yellow out of C, M, and Y, we turn on Y, but we also have to make sure that we turn off C and M. In RGB, the opposite system, we turn on R and G, and we also have to turn off B.

C	0%	100%	R
M	0%	100%	G
Y	100%	0%	B
(K)	0%		

5.1

How to mix yellow using RGB and CMYK colors. This shows the opposing nature of the two color systems.

Try playing around with this in the color-picker window in Photoshop. Click on the foreground color to open the window, and in the RGB area enter a value of 255 for R and G, and 0 for B. The result is yellow. Then try entering 255 for R and B and the result is magenta. And entering 255 for G and B will give you cyan. So the RGB system contains C, M and Y as secondary combinations of its three primaries. Then try the same using the C, M, and Y of the CMYK area. A combination of 100% cyan and magenta will give you as close to RGB blue as you can get using pigments. It looks like a dark purple. If you enter 100% for magenta and yellow, you will get the pigment version of RGB red. It is red, but nowhere near as bright or saturated as RGB red. Lastly, try 100% of yellow and cyan. The result is the CMYK version of RGB green—a long way from RGB green, but again as close as CMYK can get. So the CMYK system also contains versions of the RGB colors as secondary combinations of its primaries, although they are fairly dull and drab when compared to the RGB versions. This means it is very tempting to use something bright, saturated and *RGB* when we create colors on-screen.

So, it is the differences between RGB and CMYK that are most important, because they are what cause the problems. The combination of 100% cyan and 100% magenta might look completely different and less interesting than pure RGB blue, which we are therefore tempted to pick instead, but it is as close as CMYK can get. Most designers do not really take that seriously enough, so they merrily send RGB colors off to the printer. The result, of course, is a total disaster.

Understanding and remembering the relative nature of color is hugely important because it keeps us aware of the bigger picture, all the time. For a designer, the bigger picture might be the whole page rather than just one of the images on it, the whole project rather than just that single page, and the entire environment in which the work will

How you perceive color

exist rather than just the process that led up to its delivery to the client.

So, what color is a green leaf in a dark room? And why is it important?

Right now, you might feel that the leaf stays green, even in the dark. If so, see if the following changes your mind.

If you think about it, the only things our eyes can see are color and shape. Both depend on light. So everything we see depends on the presence of light. So far we can all agree. But the color of what we see depends on the color of the light. A leaf only looks green if the light shining on it is white. It absorbs all the other colors and reflects green, and in our minds the green-ness and the leaf-ness somehow become one thing. But that is not accurate at all. If it were, then no matter what we did to it, the leaf would stay green. Yet if we shine a red light on it, there is no green to reflect at us, because red light does not contain a green element. Suddenly the leaf looks very dark, almost black. But the leaf itself has not changed at all. The only thing that has changed is the light, which bounces off the leaf as impartially as it does everything else within range. And there is no fundamental, inherent light source that is more valid than any other light source, despite what whole civilizations have thought about the sun up until now. It is just that we are used to the sun hanging around up above us every day, and the lights we have in our houses are designed to be similar in color. And so we have come to feel the most comfortable with the way our world appears when it is illuminated with a white-ish source of light. White light contains all the colors of the spectrum, so the objects it illuminates reflect the widest possible visible range. Things look more real to us under white light than a light of any other color, but the fact that we prefer how things look under white light is just a habit based on how we are used to seeing things. So a leaf is not *inherently* green. Or red. Or anything. It is *relative*, and it depends on other equally relative factors for all its apparently inherent character-istics, just like everything else. In the case of the green leaf, if there is no light it is impossible to talk about its color, because there is nothing present on which its color would depend.

Can you trust your eyes?

What this example shows us is that we should question what our mind does with the information our eyes send it about what is out there. Yet what about the visual image itself? Can we trust that? Probably not, because here our mind plays yet another trick on us.

For instance, imagine that you have decided to paint your living room. You look through loads of small color swatches at your local home improvement store and settle for a vivid salmon pink. When you have finished painting the room, the color looks totally different and you hate it immediately. So what happened?

When you looked at the swatch, your peripheral vision was also taking in all the other colors that were around it at the time, whereas when you are looking at four salmon pink walls there is nothing else there to dilute the experience. This is why home improvement stores also sell small tins of color so that you can paint an area big enough to give you a better idea of what your room might look like if you go ahead.

Whether you are designing a page or painting a room, you need to be aware of the effect the juxtaposition of the colors you are using creates. Try to design holistically. Even if someone looks at only a small section of the page you are designing, they are going to see the whole thing—and so should you.

A case study

N ow that the basics of RGB and CMYK have been covered, let us have a look at a practical example of the kind of problem you might encounter with them.

Some years ago, at a print shop in Cumbria, England, an excellent designer, Charlie, was asked to put together a brochure for a company which specialized in designing and building unmanned submarines. In creating a design for them, Charlie made two very big mistakes.

First mistake: Charlie decided to use two beautiful shades of blue, readily available in Photoshop, to create a full-bleed graduated tint as a background for the whole thing. This would look like an underwater shot of the ocean on which the text and all the pictures of the submarines could swim around together.

Second mistake: Charlie decided to save everybody some money and proof the job to the client on-screen rather than getting **Cromalin** proofs made. Inkjet machines were not good enough to do the job back then, and digital proofs were not yet available.

As we are obviously using CMYK to print this book I cannot actually show you the two RGB colors Charlie picked—but I can show you where he picked them and also how to see them for yourself. If you go into Photoshop and click on the foreground color chip near the foot of the "tools" window, the "color picker" window appears. The locations of the two blues are shown in the screen capture of the color picker in fig. **5.2**. In both cases, Charlie selected the area he wanted by clicking on the vertical rainbow-colored bar in the middle of the window and then by clicking in the top right of the big square of color to its left. This allowed him to pick the exact shade he wanted. The numerical RGB values for the two colors were 0-R, 0-G, 255-B for the darker blue, and 0-R, 255-G, 255-B for the lighter blue.

Then he filled the entire brochure panel with a linear graduated tint of the two shades, starting with the darker blue at the bottom and fading to the lighter blue at the top. It looked great, and he went ahead with placing the text and photographs.

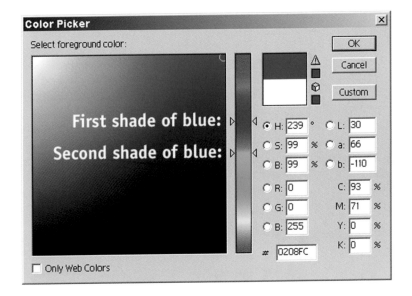

5.2

Photoshop's "color picker" window.

Unfortunately, Charlie had picked two shades of blue that do not actually exist within the CMYK range. By not bothering to run a proof, Charlie was letting the imagesetter convert all the RGB colors into CMYK as it produced the film. So, the first time anyone saw the result was when it was coming off the end of a four-color Heidelberg press at 3,000 copies per hour. It looked awful.

By not running a proof, Charlie did not save any money at all—quite the reverse, in fact—and of course it was the print shop's loss. The other problem was that it was impossible to give the client what he had seen on screen and now really wanted—because the colors could not be created using CMYK. In the end, the print shop lost the job, and Charlie very nearly lost his job as well.

Of course, if he had known what was going to happen in the transition from RGB to CMYK, Charlie could have still have started with the RGB colors but then desaturated them a bit (see chapter 16), which might have easily given him some completely acceptable choices from within the CMYK range.

Look at the CMYK percentages showing in the lower right-hand corner of fig. 5.2: 93% cyan, 71% magenta. Normally, there should be no problem printing that. But how about if we re-specify the color by entering those exact percentages in the CMYK area itself, rather than just picking a color that looks nice? And while we do it, watch what happens to the little circle that is currently up in the top right corner of the big color square on the left.

As we enter the percentages, the circle moves to a completely new position (fig. **5.3**). In addition, the color shown in the "this is your new color" area (i.e. the upper half of the rectangle which appears to the left of the "cancel" button; the lower half of it shows the color currently selected at the time you opened the color-picker window) is now displaying the color indicated by the current position of the little circle in the big square. The small triangular warning sign (that used to be just between the "new color" rectangle and the cancel button) has also vanished. That was the "out of gamut" warning. It appears only when you have chosen a color that is out of the CMYK range.

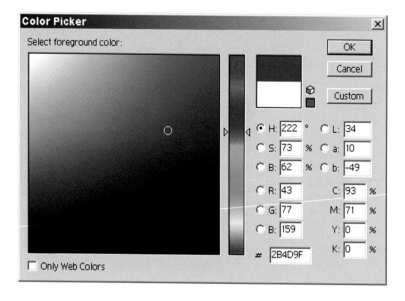

5.3
The "color-picker" window can be misleading when choosing a CMYK color.

The little square box which appears under the out-of-gamut triangle shows you the CMYK color that is closest to the RGB color you picked. Of course, you still cannot trust it to show you an accurate CMYK color, because it is still appearing on your RGB screen. Aside from that it is very small, and therefore hard to see properly. But it can be very, very different from the color you originally picked. If you click on it, it will fill the "new color" area with the same CMYK tint, and then vanish.

It is therefore very important to understand that the big colored box on the left side of the window is the *RGB* color picker, and it includes a huge range of colors beyond those available using just the CMYK pigments.

This is not only a problem for people using Photoshop—almost all the major DTP (desktop publishing) software gives you ample opportunity to pick or create RGB colors which are outside the CMYK range. Quark and PageMaker both contain RGB red, green and blue in their default color palette, with no warnings of any kind attached to them. Illustrator and CorelDraw will allow you to create blends of RGB reds, greens, and blues with no trouble at all. The problem only becomes apparent when you output the film, unless you are running a digital proof before actual film output. There is an old but accurate saying in the print industry: if you catch the problem at the artwork stage, fixing it will cost you roughly the price of a takeout lunch; at the film stage it will cost ten lunches; and if it gets onto the press, a hundred. But nowadays, lunch costs more.

How do you pick the colors you need?

It is difficult. There are useful guides out there, but sometimes it is a bit of a shot in the dark using them. Probably the most common aids to color selection are the books in the Pantone range or other tint books from a variety of sources.

As I deal specifically with Pantone Matching System (PMS) colors in chapter 15, I am not going to say much about them here. However, if you are using the Pantone Process Guide, or the Pantone Solid to Process Guide, or any other kind of tint book, read on.

The Pantone Process Guide is definitely the one to use when you are trying to create CMYK tints for a print job.

To quote Pantone, "The Pantone Process Guide displays over 3,000 CMYK color combinations on coated stock. Chromatically arranged for fast color selection, these guides are an ideal way to visualize, communicate, and control applied process colors for type, logos, borders, backgrounds, and other graphics treatments."

All you need to do is select your color from the book, read what the CMYK tint specification is, enter those values for a new color in your design software, and use it. And that is all. You do not need to worry about how it looks on-screen because you know it will print so close to the color you picked from the book that nobody will have cause for complaint.

Also, as the process guide uses all four CMYK colors it is a much more useful tool than a simple tint book, as you will see.

The Pantone Solid to Process Guide, to quote Pantone again, "shows what happens when you attempt to reproduce a solid Pantone Matching System color in four-color process printing. Although many can be successfully simulated, the majority cannot due to the limitations of the four-color process as compared to using pre-mixed inks. The fan-guide displays 1,089 solid Pantone colors on coated stock alongside their closest four-color process match. The CMYK screen values are provided for each color."

In other words, do not pick a PMS color and then expect a CMYK tint to be able to match it, because most likely it cannot.

Tint books can be both a blessing and a curse. As they come from a variety of sources they can range from being very useful (the Pantone Process Guide) to almost useless (lots of the other ones). Some printers produce their own, based on the particular levels at which they like to run CMYK work in-house. These are obviously most accurate only when you have sent your work to that particular print shop. Unfortunately, there are lots and lots of them out there.

Typically, each of the (quite large) pages in this kind of tint book is divided into many small squares of color. The row down the left side is a light shade of magenta—5% or 10%—and as you continue across the page, each row increases in density until the very right hand column is a solid 100%. The same is true of cyan, but this will start with a light tint at the top of the page and gradually increase to a 100% solid on the bottom row. The result is a very light tint in the square at top left and a very dense color in the square at bottom right. This first page has no yellow whatsoever. On page 2, all the squares are overprinted with a yellow tint of perhaps 5%. On page 3, it is increased to 10%. On page 4, it is 15%— and so on until at the end of the book it is a 100% overlay. So, you have all the possible combinations of cyan, magenta and yellow in increments of 5% or 10% all the way up to 100% of each. Incidentally, try not to select any color where the combination of the three ink densities adds up to more than 270%, or you will probably run into "picking" (see chapter 9).

Unfortunately, most tint books are set up without black appearing, and this can lead to serious problems. For an in-depth description, see "GCR in action" in chapter 9.

When black is involved in a tint book it tends to be in one of two ways. The first is when you get an envelope with the book containing a piece of clear film showing squares containing different strengths of a black tint. The idea is to lay it down over one of the color swatches in the book to see the combination of the two. Right from the start, the addition of the film clouds the appearance of the colors, and it becomes cloudier and more yellow as it ages.

The second way is when each of the (already quite small) color swatches in the book has a border along two sides on which a few (even smaller) blocks of black tint are overprinted (fig. **5.4**):

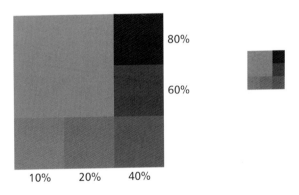

5.4

In a typical tint book, color swatches are overlayed with a block of black tint. The larger square is an enlargement. The small square on the right is much closer to actual swatch sizes.

80%

60%

10%   20%   40%

As you can see, the size of the black overprinted areas is so small that it is extremely difficult to tell what the color really looks like.

Neither of the above methods really works if you wish to select colors that include black. In that event you would be much better off using the Pantone Process Guide.

Some color psychology

What would you say if I asked you to pick a color to use as a headline in an ad—a color that could not be ignored, that literally forced people to take notice of it?

The chances are you would say "bright red."

But why? What is it that is so special about red? Why are all our stop lights, danger signals, fire equipment and so on painted red? Even though we probably cannot explain quite why that should be the case, we still somehow recognize that a light green, for example, just would not work the same way.

Here is a possible, but plausible, reason.

Our eyes contain two different kinds of light-sensing cells: "rod" and "cone" cells. Rod cells only pick up light intensity and do not transmit any color information at all. Cone cells only pick up color—but they are selective. Some pick up red, some pick up green, and some pick up blue. And they are not all present in the same ratio.

Imagine how things might have been 50,000 years ago, when we were physically just about the same as we are now but had not made any technological advances beyond the use of basic tools. Then consider what the natural environment would have been like. There would not have been many things that looked blue other than the sky and the ocean. The people who lived back then did not—could not—make use of either. There were no boats or planes. So blue was there, but it was not very important in terms of day-to-day survival.

Green, on the other hand, was important. If there was lots of green around, it meant that things were growing, which in turn meant that there was a source of food available, either from the green stuff itself or from other animals that were eating it. So it was very important but it was not a problem.

How about red? Strangely enough, there are actually very few things in the natural environment that are red. Sunsets and sunrises, and some flowers and berries—and since many red berries are poisonous, the ability to recognize red was important. But generally, if a lot of red was visible, it usually meant somebody had cut themselves or that something was on fire. So red was not only important, it could trigger immediate action in a way no other color ever did. So it came to mean "pay attention, right now" and has become particularly associated with urgency and danger.

The ratio between the cone cells, red to green to blue, is 40:20:1. So we have actually evolved to able to see, recognize and respond to red better than for any other color.

However, if you want to create a headline that is not particularly noticeable at all, try a nice pale blue.

CHAPTER 6

Getting the Most out of Your Monitor

A monitor checklist

In order to determine how close your monitor is to telling you the truth, you need to have some printed images as well as the actual image files that were used to produce the film and/or plates from which they were printed. However, before using the method described below, or any other calibration method, first run through the following monitor checklist:

1) Are you using a standard desktop (cathode ray tube—CRT) or good-quality flat-screen monitor? If you are using a low-quality or slightly faulty monitor, this chapter will not be of much help to you.

2) If you have either the "monitor setup" utility supplied with PageMaker 6 for Windows or the Knoll Gamma control panel (it came with Photoshop 4) for the Mac OS, remove it. These are now obsolete, according to Adobe.

3) If you have a CRT monitor, make sure it has been on for at least half an hour so that everything is completely warmed up.

4) Make sure your monitor is displaying "thousands of colors" (i.e. 16-bit) or more.

5) Do you have a background image of some distracting and not at all relevant image displayed on your desktop that is visible while you use Photoshop? If so, get rid of it. Replace it with a nice neutral gray, created using equal R, G, and B values of 128. On a scale of 256 shades, "128" represents a completely neutral 50% gray, which is exactly what you need for a background instead of whatever you have there now.

6) If your monitor has digital controls which allow you to choose the white point, try starting out with it set to 6500 K .

7) Many users will consider all the above to be important while completely ignoring one of the absolutely most important points of all: the lighting in your working environment. You have to control this if you possibly can, otherwise any other calibration you do will be compromised. Lights can be turned on or off. The sun goes up and comes back down again. Some days are overcast, some are bright. Every one of these variables will affect how everything in your field of vision appears—including the images displayed on your monitor. If you are serious about getting it right in print, you will aim to have as few variables as possible getting in the way. Figure out the kind of lighting that will work best for you, and try to stick with it.

8) Monitors get old, so you should recalibrate things every two or three months. If you find that you can no longer set it the way you used to, and need to, then unfortunately it is time for a new monitor.

Hopefully you already have, or can get hold of (if the printer or repro house did the final scans for you) some images that have actually been included in a Quark or PageMaker file that has been printed on an offset press. They do not have to be the full-size versions—it is fine to use lower-resolution copies. The important thing is that the color has not been adjusted at all since they went off for printing. Hopefully you also have a representative printed copy.

Holding the printed copy in your hand, and with the image that created the film for it opened in Photoshop (do not use Quark or PageMaker, etc., because they do not display CMYK images very well), adjust the settings on your monitor until the two are as close as you can possibly make them. The more images you can do this with, the better. When in doubt, I open up about ten small images and work on the monitor adjustments while they are all right in front of me. You may find that while most of the color range is reasonably accurate, one area may be more or less saturated than you are happy with. If so, you will need to estimate roughly how much lighter or darker a particular color is, and then you can try re-calibrating your monitor using Adobe Gamma, which comes with Photoshop. To find it on a PC, go to "start/control panel/ adobe gamma." On a Mac it is under the "chooser/control" menu, unless it is switched off, in which case you will have to do a search for it. Or, if they are available, try adjusting the individual RGB color levels on your monitor. Of course the difficulty is that if you add more blue, it will have a similar effect to taking away yellow, which can very easily disturb the balance of the rest of the image.

Usually there is a degree of compromise, but that is all we can really hope for. It is just not possible to completely rely on your monitor for accurate color. Fortunately, the kind of mix in a typical continuous-tone image means it is slightly less susceptible to variations in appearance than an area of flat color, where a slight difference can radically affect the result. And, fortunately, the flat areas are the easy ones to fix. Therefore, while not being able to completely trust what you see on screen, you can

Backwards calibration

at least calibrate things to the point of being able to trust the mid-tone information that your monitor is showing you. You cannot use it to visually judge the highlights, or the shadows, and especially the exact colors—but for the general appearance, and the overall lightness or darkness of the mid-tone range, you can open up an image on screen and know that as far as those qualities are concerned, it is extremely close to how the printed result will look.

I use backwards calibration to get accurate color output from the print shop without having to trust my monitor. To do the same, you will need a good tint book and a good desktop inkjet printer, or some other way of producing color prints of your work.

If you do not have a reasonably modern inkjet printer—and by reasonably modern I mean one that can produce images at a resolution of 720 dpi or more—then you are missing out on a very useful piece of equipment (see chapter 12 for more about inkjet resolution). These printers are amazingly cheap, especially in letter size (US) or A4 (UK) formats, and their high-resolution prints, when they are on the right paper, are superb.

The manufacturers of inkjet printers tend to sell them at very slightly more than cost, making them look like an extremely reasonable purchase. Then they truly stick it to you for the ink. I am reliably informed that, weight for weight, inkjet ink is more expensive than gold.

The idea is that you can use the injket printer to generate a print you are happy with, then use the tint book and the print to figure out what color specifications you actually need in the image on screen.

For this example, let us say you have designed a book cover.

It is all there on your monitor, and it looks great. Then you print it out and you are not quite so happy. So you have to adjust the color and continue to print it out until you have a print of a book cover you will be proud to include in your portfolio. This is the one you are going to show the client as a final design draft.

Print out another copy and cut little holes in it so that you can put it down over the pages in the tint book. Move it around until you find the square that is the closest color match to it, then adjust the tint specifications in the software until they match those shown in the tint book.

This is very easy to do when creating images in Adobe Illustrator or CorelDraw, where you have to decide what color to make everything anyway. It is much harder to achieve using Adobe Photoshop, where you are very often working with continuous-tone images—but with practice, it can be done—especially if your design allows you to make selections of certain areas and adjust them without disturbing things in the rest of the image. Use the individual channel settings in the "levels" and/or "curves" windows after placing markers on the image with the color sampler tool (see chapter 5). Then, the "info" window can give you before/after information as you make adjustments. If you have previously calibrated your monitor using the method described below, you should easily be able to tell if your image is getting out of hand.

As for the areas that backwards calibration cannot reach—the highlights and shadows—these can fortunately be calibrated very accurately indeed using the method described in the next chapter.

CHAPTER 7

Calibrating a Grayscale Image

Dealing with highlights and shadows

Here is a very simple method which takes all the worry out of trying to set image highlights and shadows properly. With a little experience, you will confidently be able to handle this kind of calibration in any kind of image without relying on anyone's help.

But first, why do you need to be particularly concerned with the highlights and shadows? The answer lies in understanding the nature of the offset-printing process. While you are working on a digital file, everything is perfect—as far as transfer of the data is concerned. You could copy the file back and forth from one system to another again and again, and so long as nothing actually went wrong, you would end up with exactly the same file that you started with. However, once you get out into the "real" world, it is a different matter. Imagine making a copy of a video tape. Then a copy of the copy. Then a copy of the copy of the copy, and so on. Pretty soon, there would be no video any more, just garbage. Each time you make a non-digital transfer, you lose a percentage of the quality of the original, and the problem is compounded with each subsequent transfer. When you send your file off to the printer, the first stage of transfer—creating the film—is still digital. But the next, from film to plate, is a physical transfer (and therefore an imperfect transfer, with data loss) from one medium to another. The next transfer, from plate to blanket, is also a physical transfer, and also imperfect. But the biggest change in the data occurs when the blanket transfers the image to the paper. That is because, as well as being a physical transfer, paper tends to allow ink to absorb into it and spread along the fibres from which it is made. Obviously, some papers—newsprint, for example—will do this a lot, while others, such as coated papers, hardly do it at all.

The result of all this is generally referred to as "dot gain." To be really accurate, dot gain actually refers to the increase in density of a 50% dot on a piece of film compared to the resulting density when it is finally printed on the paper. However, in terms of effect on the image, it is not only the mid-tones that undergo change; in the shadow areas, the big dots also get bigger, and in the highlights, the small dots get smaller.

The effect of this on the appearance of the highlights and shadows is very detrimental. If you started with an image where the tone range ran all the way from black through to white, then after it had been printed the tone within much of the highlights and shadows simply would not exist any more. Highlights would have burned out to white, shadows would have filled in to black. Typically this means that your image now has holes in the sky and holes in the ground.

It may be obvious or it may be quite subtle. It may be quite difficult, looking at the result, to pin down exactly why it looks wrong. But instinctively, you know that something is just not quite right with the picture, and your natural tendency is to leave it behind and go on to something else—the next article, picture, whatever. Mentally, you turn your back on it. Which, if the image is part of an advertisement, intended to make you buy something, is a marketing disaster.

Remember, all you need to be is convincing—and holes in the sky or the ground are not convincing.

You do not need to worry about the mid-tones yet. If you have calibrated your workflow using the method described in the previous chapter, they can be fixed along the way as you deal with the highlights and shadows.

What you have to do is squeeze the entire tonal range slightly and thus artificially flatten the contrast. By deliberately flattening the contrast in the image, you are making the smallest dots slightly larger, and the largest dots slightly smaller. During the printing process, all will undergo dot gain, thus getting respectively smaller and larger but without burning out or filling in. The amount by which you need to do this primarily depends on the kind of paper you intend to print on. Is it a high-quality coated paper or newsprint? Will the ink stay more or less in place, or will it spread out along the fibres of the paper as soon as it touches it? If printing on a coated paper, you will need to allow about a 5% buffer zone at either end. For uncoated paper, 8% to 12%. For newsprint, it starts at around 12% but can be as much as 20%. These are approximate dot-gain values for sheet-fed printing. Web-offset values can be considerably higher.

Creating a dot-gain test strip

Of course, dot gain also depends on the quality of the printing machine and the person running it. Try asking the printers at what point—i.e. at what percentage—the shadow dots will fill in and the highlight dots burn out, given the paper you have chosen and the press they plan to run the job on. If you are lucky, the printers will already have a pretty good idea of what will happen, and might even have run some tests of their own. If not, and you plan on using them for a lot of your work, suggest that it might be to their advantage in the long run if they do some calibration tests for you. You will need to supply them with a "dot-gain test strip" which you can easily make as a simple **TIFF** or **EPS** file. To create one of these, draw a series of twenty-one small squares, something like the example shown (fig. **7.1**). You can create these in many applications, but if you use (for example) Illustrator or CorelDraw, you can then open the result in Photoshop and check that the gray percentages have not changed. If you get some of the color-management options appearing as you open the file, check the notes at the end of chapter 10 to help you decide what to do. (Do not miss these—they could be very important!) Fill the central box with a 50% gray. For the ten boxes to the left, fill the first with a 1% tint, the second with a 2% tint, and so on up to 10%. For the right-hand boxes, start at 90% and go all the way up to 99%.

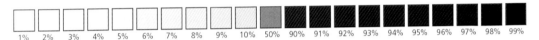

7.1

A calibration strip which, when printed, will tell you where the highlight and shadow dots burn out or fill in, as well as giving you a dot-gain factor for a 50% tint.

Ask the printers to position it outside the live area on a print job running the same paper stock that you plan to use (or something very similar, if that is not possible) and on the same press. If you plan to use the printers a lot, suggest that they run it on as many variations of paper and press as they can for a while. Soon you will have a very accurate picture of what will happen on different presses using a wide range of papers. Ask the printers to check the 50% value of each sample with a **densitometer**. The difference between the original 50% tint and the value shown by the densitometer is the dot-gain factor. Look at the shadow and highlight squares with a magnifying glass and see where the dots burned out and filled in. Those are the values you have to compensate for with calibration.

If there is a medium to high percentage of burn-out in one of the squares, you should adjust to the next higher value for the highlights and the next lower value for the shadows. If, for example, lots of the 4% highlight dots did not make it, but only a few of the 5% dots vanished, you will have to adjust the tone range to allow for a 4% loss at that end of the scale. Therefore the lightest tint in the image after calibration will be 5%. If, at the other end of the spectrum, lots of the tiny white dots still show in the 93% square but the 94% square is almost completely filled in to black, you will have to adjust for a 7% loss at that end, and therefore the darkest pixels that should be left in your image will be 93%.

This will take care of the highlights and shadows beautifully.

A practical example of grayscale calibration

n Adobe Photoshop, open the image you want to calibrate (see fig. **7.2** for my example) and also the "info" window (it is under the "window" menu). Use the color-sampler tool, which looks like this: [icon]. (It is under the eye-dropper tool, which looks like this: [icon]. If you click and hold down on it you will see the flyout palette. The color-sampler tool is the middle one of the three). With the color-sampler tool selected, you can click on the image and place up to four markers. These will show up in the info window and tell you the density of pixels underneath them as a gray percentage. Better still, as you make adjustments to the image, they will give you live "before" and "after" information. The idea is to place one marker on the darkest pixels and another on the lightest and then adjust the image until both are showing the percentages that you want.

7.2

In this example, the level of contrast is quite flat and the tonal range stops short of either black or white. This picture clearly needs some help.

Before starting this process, make sure that your info window is showing you grayscale information ("k" values) in the top-left quadrant. If not, click on the "options" arrow, select "palette options" and tell the first color readout to show actual color.

Now open the "threshold" window by choosing "image/adjust/threshold" (fig. **7.3**). The image will immediately change, becoming black and white (fig. **7.4**).

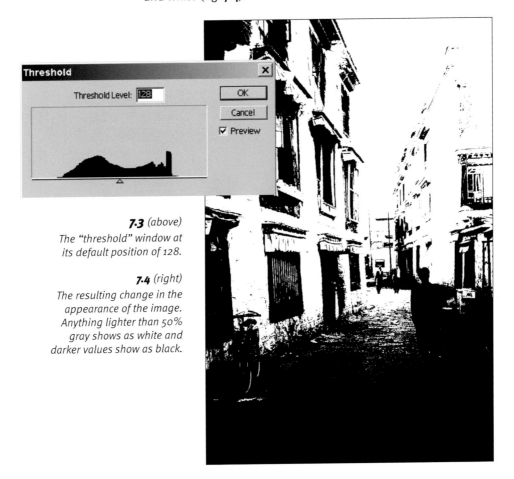

7.3 (above)
The "threshold" window at its default position of 128.

7.4 (right)
The resulting change in the appearance of the image. Anything lighter than 50% gray shows as white and darker values show as black.

Under the "pixel pile" histogram, which shows the range of tone currently present in the image, is a slider. The mid-point position of the slider (the threshold) indicates that all the areas in the image showing as

59

black are to the left of the slider and therefore darker than a 50% gray, whereas areas showing in white are to the right of the slider and therefore lighter than 50%. The default position of the slider when you open the threshold window is at "128," which is the mid-point of a 256-shade grayscale image.

Move the slider towards the left-hand end of the pixel pile (fig. **7.5**). Gradually, the black areas in the image shrink (fig. **7.6**). The further you move the slider, the fewer areas are left which are darker than the threshold level. When you are close to the left-hand end of the pixel pile only the very darkest areas in the image are left showing.

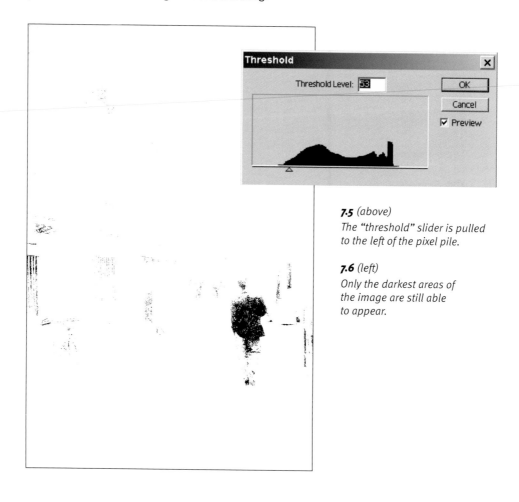

7.5 *(above)*
The "threshold" slider is pulled to the left of the pixel pile.

7.6 *(left)*
Only the darkest areas of the image are still able to appear.

Take a good look—so that you can remember where they are—and then click "cancel." Now you know roughly where to place your first marker. Move the cursor around in that area, and as you do so, watch the numbers change in the "k" area of the info window. Find the darkest pixel you can, and then click on it. A new area appears at the foot of the info window showing the "k" value of the pixel under the marker you have just placed.

Then repeat the process, but this time move the slider to the right (fig. **7.7**). This time, the last areas left visible indicate the lightest pixels in the image (fig. **7.8**). As before, click "cancel" and place a second marker on the lightest pixel you can find.

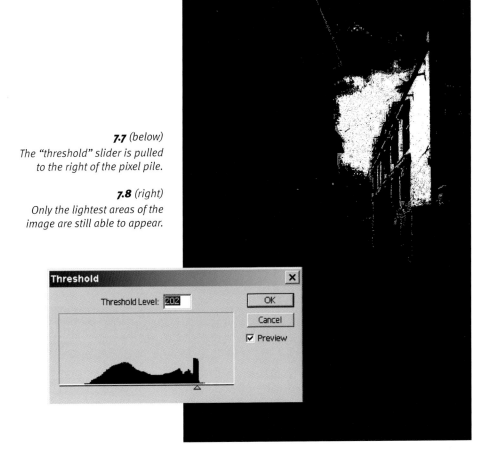

7.7 (below)
The "threshold" slider is pulled to the right of the pixel pile.

7.8 (right)
Only the lightest areas of the image are still able to appear.

If the marker does not land exactly where you wanted it to, you can either grab it and drag it to a new position, or delete it ("alt-" or "option-click" on it) and try again. Of course, if you want, you can zoom in until the individual pixels are visible, then it is easy to position the markers more accurately. The info window should now look something like fig. **7.9**.

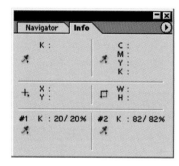

7.9
The "info" window showing "before" and "after" marker information prior to any calibration adjustment.

Now click on "image/adjust/levels." As in the threshold window, the levels-window histogram (the black mound) shows relatively how many pixels of each shade of gray, from black on the far left through to white on the far right, are represented in the image (fig. **7.10**). If the mound does not extend all the way to the left and/or right, it indicates that the image lacks contrast at one or both ends of the range. In this example, it confirms what we already knew from setting up the markers in the info window—there is nothing darker than 82% gray and nothing lighter than 20%.

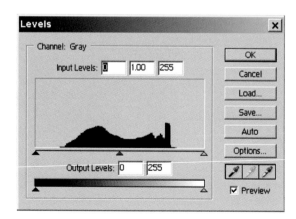

7.10
The "levels" window prior to any adjustment.

Now for the actual calibration.

In order to create a 5% "gap" at either end of the scale we need to pull the information in the image further out towards solid black and white to leave the darkest point set at 95% and the brightest at 5%.

If the information displayed is similar to the example shown in fig. 7.10, in which the pixel pile stops short of either end of the scale, then the adjustment can be made simply by pulling the black and/or white point arrows (situated just below the histogram, at either end) in towards the pixel pile. As you move them, the info window will update to show the new values for the pixels tracked by your color-sampler markers. When they get to 95% and 5%, the info and levels window will look similar to the examples shown in figs **7.11** and **7.12**.

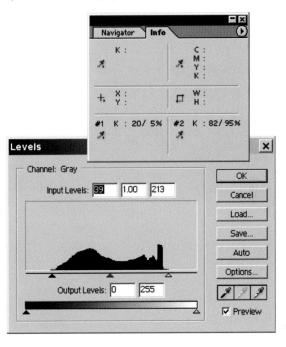

7.11 (above) and 7.12 (right)
The "info" window updates as changes are made to the "levels" histogram using the black and white point arrows. In this example, the new shadow value is 95% and the new highlight value is 5%.

NOTE: If the information shown in the input-levels histogram already goes right out to either the black point on the far left or the white point on the far right, you can instead drag the arrows situated at either end of the output-levels slider (that is the area under the histogram filled with a graduated gray tint) until the info window tells you that the correct percentage of adjustment has been made at both ends of the scale.

These arrows can be used to "squash" the entire histogram from one or both ends without cutting off any of the pixel information. Alternatively, you could make the adjustment using the numerical "output levels" boxes. The histogram represents 256 shades of gray, therefore a 1% change equals 2.56 shades. A 5% change would therefore be 12.8 shades, but as we can only adjust in whole numbers, the closest we can get is 13. Therefore you would change the 0 to 13 and the 255 to 242.

If you click "OK" to accept these changes, the calibration of the image —at least as far as the highlights and shadows are concerned—is complete. The image should now show a similar improvement to the example shown in fig. **7.13**.

7.13
*The final image
after calibration.*

And that is basically it.

To see how Photoshop has dealt with distributing the existing gray levels between the 5% and 95% points to which you have just constrained them, go back into levels. The histogram should now look something like fig. **7.14**.

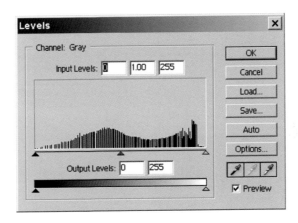

7.14

The new spread of tone values in the calibrated image. The vertical white gaps represent shades of gray that are no longer present.

The white gaps showing between the vertical black lines are just that: shades which are not represented in your image. Unless these gaps are wide, it is very unlikely to be a problem, as we can actually get away with far fewer shades of gray than you might think, and still be convincing. For example, fig. **7.15** shows two apparently identical sections of the image. One of them shows the same number of shades as the original image, distributed evenly between 5% and 95%. Next to it is a copy in which the number of shades of gray has been restricted to 75—also distributed evenly between 5% and 95%. Can you tell which one is the restricted sample?

Remember—each image is different and you should not make the same blind adjustment to everything. Your image may, for example, include "specular" highlights such as the reflection off a chrome bumper, or lights in a night scene. These *should* be completely white, and will not look right if you have filled them with a 5% highlight dot. Similarly, a photograph of a foggy scene is unlikely to contain very dense shadow tones. These will look much too dark if you pull them back out to a value of 95% black.

7.15
The one on the right has 75 shades.

Adding contrast

f you decide that, despite your calibration of all the highlights and shadows, the image still needs a bit of extra "punch," you may want to add more contrast. Please, please, please do *not* use "image/adjust/brightness and contrast." In fact, it is really better if you just forget that particular tool completely, unless you actually want to burn out what were previously light grays to white, and fill in dark grays to black. This is not, as you may think, what you do when you **posterize** an image. Posterizing is where you restrict the image to displaying a particular number of shades of gray. That is different—and very effective, although easily over-used. The brightness and contrast adjustments will only do that at the top and bottom of the tonal range—which does produce more contrast, but does so at the expense of the shades shown in those areas. Once you have wiped out those areas of information, you might never get them back.

To show you what I mean, here is an example.

Let us take the calibrated image and use the levels window to apply exactly the same kind of adjustment that "brightness and contrast" would give you.

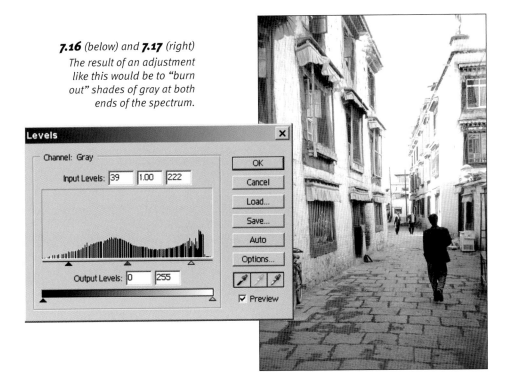

7.16 *(below) and **7.17** (right)*
The result of an adjustment like this would be to "burn out" shades of gray at both ends of the spectrum.

As you can see in fig. **7.16** I have pulled the black and white point arrows in so that they are underneath the pixel information. What this means is that the parts of the histogram which are outside those arrows no longer hold shades of gray. Instead, everything to the right of the white point arrow is now white, and everything to the left of the black point arrow is now black. The result in the image (fig. **7.17**) would be a much greater degree of contrast—but it is at the expense of all those shades of gray which were left outside when the arrows were moved. If I had also pulled the 50% arrow to the left, I would have added brightness as well.

If you want to add contrast intelligently, then what you really need is "image/adjust/curves," and this is what you do.

Click on the diagonal line at the center point (fig. **7.18**). This places an "anchor" (A), with which you can pull the line out towards either the top left or bottom right corners of the window, into a convex or concave curve. This is just like moving the mid-point slider in the levels window; pull it one way, and the mid-tones get darker. Pull it the other, and they get lighter. If you need to lighten or darken the mid-tones, go ahead and pull—but otherwise, all you need is an anchor point on the line. If you should decide that you do not want a particular anchor point, just click on it and drag it off the square. Click again halfway between your center point and the bottom left end of the line (B), and pull slightly down and to the right. This pulls the whole line into a slight "S" curve as it rotates around the anchor point.

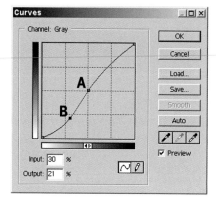

7.18

The "curves" window set to increase contrast in an image, but without the losing any of the original shades of gray.

By doing this, you pull all the "lighter-than-50%" tones into a new configuration that makes them brighter in the upper-mid range; at the same time, you push the "darker-than-50%" tones, making them darker in the lower-mid range. The overall effect is to add brightness and contrast to the image without burning out a single one of the highlight and shadow tones in the original. However, if you pull too hard, you will "flat-line" the tone range at one or both ends of the spectrum, and that is when the information burns out.

So, now you can adjust the mid-tones through "backwards calibration" of your monitor (see chapter 6), and trust them; and calibrate the highlights and shadows within an image, and trust them. So you are well on the way to never again waking up at 3 o'clock in the morning worrying about how your grayscale images are going to look!

CHAPTER 8

Bitmaps and Pixel Depth

Why are there 256 shades in a grayscale image?

In the previous chapter, the number 256 was mentioned in relation to the number of shades of gray possible in a Photoshop grayscale image. So why is it 256 and not 100? Surely we measure tint density as a percentage? While that is true, computers have brought new ways of doing things along with them as they have revolutionized the graphics industry over the past few years.

One of these differences has been a whole new approach to the construction of images. Previously, the use of a screen, positioned between the film and the image projected onto it, led to the production of a conventional halftone: a grid of round dots of different sizes, but all of the same color. Seen from a distance, we do not see the dots. Instead, we see the visual mix of the dots plus the paper showing through between them, as various shades (see chapter 1). Pure illusion, but it works.

On the computer, the illusion is different. Images are displayed as solid masses of pixels, each one a small square, and there is no space between them at all. In a single image they are all the same size and they can display many different colors. Just how many colors they can display depends on their **bit depth**, i.e. the amount of digital space they occupy on your computer.

To confuse the issue further, your monitor displays these pixels by breaking them up into very small dots (a typical CRT monitor has a "dot pitch," or dot size, of around 0.28 mm), but let us not worry about that particular illusion for now.

The simplest kind of image we can display is called a "bitmap" in Photoshop and is made up of just two colors. In fact, the word "bitmap" can actually refer to any image made up of pixels, but technical accuracy does not seem to have bothered those responsible for some of the terminology we use today. For example, we generally think of a dot as "round," and yet when we talk about pixels—which are square, of course—we refer to their density in terms of "dots per inch." Then, when we are talking about the round dots which end up on the film, the plate, the blanket and eventually the paper, we are much less likely to refer to them as dots and more likely to talk about them collectively as a "line screen," referring to the number of lines of dots there are to the inch. Small surprise, then, that there is some confusion out there. Let us not even think about the kind of dots you get out of an inkjet printer—yet.

Getting back to our simple bitmap, although the two colors can be any two colors, at their most basic level the pixels are either in a state of being completely on, in which case they are white, or completely off, in which case they are black. These pixels are called "1-bit deep," and as such they can display just these two states, each of which creates the appropriate color.

The next level up is 8-bit. Now, there is no reason why we could not have 2-bit, 3-bit, 4-bit and so on—but why bother? For example, if we had a 2-bit image, it could display 2 x 2 states: in other words, four shades of gray. So we would have 0%, 33%, 67% and 100%, which is not especially useful. Instead, the next logical step is for an image that can display enough shades between black and white to produce a really good image, hence 8-bit (which in fact provides rather more shades than are really necessary.)

Each of the 8 bits contributes two states to the equation. It is a multiplier, so there are 2 x 2 x 2 x 2 x 2 x 2 x 2 x 2 potential states available for the color display of each pixel—and that is why there are 256 shades of gray in a Photoshop grayscale image. (**NOTE**: If we really want to display fewer shades, we can always use the "posterize" command and pick any number between 256 and 2.)

Pixel depth in color images

The next step up in image complexity is color. There are several different formats of color image, and the number of colors they can display depends either on how many channels they comprise or whether they are indexed color, i.e. **GIF** format.

GIF images have no place in the printing industry and are strictly for on-screen viewing such as in web sites. Indexed color can show a maximum of 256 colors which can come from anywhere in the entire RGB range rather than having to all be shades of the same hue. If the colors are **dithered**, i.e. pixels of one color are scattered throughout a patch of another color, they visually merge to create the appearance of a color that is not actually present as one of the 256. Because of this ability, they can appear to be very convincing "full color" continuous-tone images on screen. So convincing, in fact, that you cannot tell just by looking at your monitor whether the image is GIF, **JPEG**, TIFF, or EPS format, or whether it is actually seriously compromised in terms of potential print quality.

If you do have to use a GIF image, then it needs to be converted into an acceptable format before it can be printed, and even then it is probably not going to be great because of having been constrained to 256 colors. However, occasionally there are ways to get there—see chapters 11 and 12 for some suggestions on how to turn a GIF or lower-quality JPEG image into something that will print as a convincing color image.

In a 24-bit RGB color image (which is the most common format produced by desktop scanners and digital cameras) there are three separate "channels," each one holding an 8-bit image. (A channel is the part of an image that holds all the information for any one of the component colors.) When they are displayed simultaneously, the color each one contains becomes transparent, thus allowing all their overlapping color combinations to be seen. (They can also be looked at individually, in which case it is usually more useful to view them as grayscale images, especially if you are considering changing an RGB image into grayscale format—see "Useful grayscale options" in chapter 16.) Thus the three channels together are potentially able to display all the resulting color combinations. This means that each pixel can display a mix combining any one of the 256 shades of red, plus any one of the 256 shades of green, plus any one of the 256 shades of blue—in other words, any one of 16,777,216 colors.

Now consider what the addition of yet another channel does to this number, since in a CMYK image yet another grayscale map is added. Thus, our 16.7 million is multiplied again by 256, giving us a potential range of 4,294,967,200 colors. This is clearly more colors than we can ever distinguish between. Even the most accomplished painter who spends a lot of time considering color might only be able to distinguish between 20–30,000 of them. Fortunately, however, even though our computers offer us more colors than we can ever distinguish between, it is not a problem—just think of it as an advantage that we cannot actually use.

Someone once tried to sell me a scanner based on its ability to produce 48-bit CMYK images—lovely, no doubt, but pointless. That is 12 bits per channel. Even in an RGB image, a channel depth of 12 bits would allow each pixel in a single channel to display any one of 2 x 2 x 2 x 2 x 2 x 2 x 2 x 2 x 2 x 2 x 2 x 2, or 4,096 colors. Multiply that by itself three times (because it is a three-channel image) and you have nearly 69 billion colors, which is pretty silly. In CMYK it is even sillier: 281 thousand billion.

The important information about any scanner is much more likely to be contained in the answer to the following question: what is its optical scanning resolution? At what resolution can it scan before it starts **interpolating** the image resolution, i.e. spreading the same information over a progressively larger and larger number of pixels? The optical resolution is what will allow you to pick up detail that will otherwise get left behind, so obviously it is extremely important—and much more important than having oodles of colors that you can not even distinguish between. Decent optical resolution starts at around 1200 dpi, and these days even a cheap scanner is capable of giving you an RGB image which you can probably turn into a good four-color separation, so long as you know how to do the calibration (see chapter 6).

Given that the range of color in RGB is larger than in that of CMYK, it is perhaps surprising that a CMYK image can hold a greater number of colors than the same image in RGB. This is due to confusing the difference between the range of colors within the two color spaces with the mathematical limitations imposed on digital images of both types.

The key factor here is that the number of colors potentially available in either format depends only upon the number of color channels in the image and the bit-depth of those channels. If we compare a CMYK image with four 8-bit channels with an RGB image with only three 8-bit channels, clearly the CMYK image must have the potential to display more colors. That potential is a purely physical limitation imposed by the way the software deals with things. It has nothing whatsoever to do with how many colors actually exist in either system—which, perhaps confusing the issue slightly further, is infinite in both cases: but only because in theory there is no limit to the number of shades you can divide a color into. In practice, the range is larger in RGB. RGB contains almost every CMYK color, but CMYK does not come even close to containing every RGB color. If it did, there would be nothing to discuss—and many fewer problems!

CHAPTER 9

Calibrating Color Images

Getting started

We have already covered two of the most important calibration methods: backwards calibration for the mid-tones (see chapter 6) and grayscale calibration for the highlights and shadows (see chapter 7).

When faced with trying to calibrate a color image, you may be tempted to just let someone else take care of it. Do not be put off. If you can calibrate grayscale, you can definitely calibrate color, especially if you have a reasonably good monitor and a tint book. If you need a tint book, talk to a few print shops. If they get the idea that you are a busy graphic designer looking for a reliable printer, they will try to be very helpful. Good print shops update their Pantone references every so often and might have one or two slightly older ones lying around. They will probably not have faded very much and the new ones are quite expensive (see chapter 15).

The main thing you need for good color calibration is confidence. I know graphic designers who, after years of saying how much they would like to do their own scanning, are still getting it all done by their repro house or printer because they do not think they can do it themselves.

Remember, it is unlikely that you will have to jump straight in at the deep end. Assuming right now that you do not know how to calibrate anything and that you want to end up calibrating everything, let us take it one step at a time. Start small—let your first attempt be a small image that is not fraught with problems to begin with. Nobody will notice if you end up doing a reasonable job. This may sound odd, since you would normally want somebody to notice if you did a reasonable job, but not in this case. If someone notices what you did, it will either be because it is just wonderful, or just awful. If you are only going to start with a small image on a page that also contains larger, more important images, it is unlikely anyone is going to appreciate the quality of calibration on the postage-stamp-sized image you worked on. If nobody notices anything, you have won—you will have been convincing. Eventually, you may want people to notice, but for now be content with anonymity.

Also, do not imagine that the repro house/print shop is populated by beings with god-like calibration capabilities. The chances are they are using similar equipment to yours and doing similar things with it. Also, the chances are that they are much less concerned with doing a good job on your scans than you are, so once you get the hang of things you will make a better job of your work than they will.

Gray component replacement

Fortunately, with color images, Adobe Photoshop is extremely helpful. The bad news is that the ways in which it is most helpful are somewhat cutting-edge (see chapter 10, "Color-Management Systems") and not easy for even quite experienced users to understand. However, the great thing about the following calibration method is that it will produce good results for you without requiring you to venture into the more difficult and arcane area of Photoshop's color settings.

First, it is necessary to set up your work station properly. On a PC screen, all the software packages have opaque backgrounds of bland, screen-filling neutral gray. Mac users have transparent backgrounds in nearly all their software so that the delightful scene they have loaded as their desktop image is more-or-less visible all the time. For calibration to work, images need a surrounding area of neutral, 50% RGB gray, so you need to generate an image in which you have selected 128 as the numerical value for each of the three channels and use it as your background. The number 128 represents the halfway point along a scale running from zero to 256, which therefore means each color will be displayed at a strength of 50%. Whenever all three colors are displayed at equal densities, the result is a neutral gray of that percentage.

When you calibrate grayscale images, one of the main things you have to watch is that the shadows do not fill in. With color images, you do not really need to worry about this because in a color image the shadow density is carried by four colors instead of one. Even in very dark areas, it is very unlikely that all four colors—or even three of them—will be present at a density higher than 80%. Despite that, you are still going to get good strong shadows in most images, but without any of them actually filling in. This is because Photoshop (usually) protects you from a problem called "combined ink density" that most other software will allow you to fall right into. That is simply a figure produced by adding together the percentages at which each of the four colors is present in any particular pixel. In practice, if your combined ink density reaches around 250%, you are getting dangerously close to what is called the "maximum ink density"

—which, when reached, means that the ink will not stick to the paper any more because there is already too much ink on it. This results in a phenomenon known in the trade as **picking**, and it makes a horrible sound like a whole bunch of people peeling their hands away from semi-dry paint simultaneously. To avoid this problem in the other software programs, see "creating and using a rich black" in chapter 14.

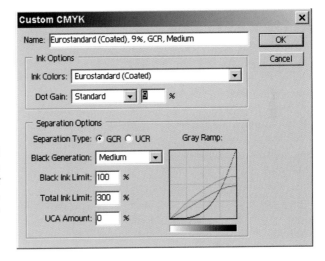

9.1

The "gray ramp": a graph displaying the level at which black ink replaces C, M, and Y within an image.

Photoshop applies "gray component replacement" (GCR) as part of a "color-management system" (CMS) when cyan, magenta, and yellow are all present at fairly high densities within a single pixel. It removes them in a predetermined ratio (fig. **9.1**) and replaces them with black. It can do this because, at that ratio, C, M, and Y combine to produce a neutral shade of gray. The higher the density of C, M, and Y, the more the replacement occurs. As well as cutting down on the total ink requirements, this helps to ensure that not a single pixel hits maximum ink density. (There is more about color-management systems in chapter 10.)

GCR in action

A few years ago I was the production manager of a medium-size print shop in the US. One of our clients regularly sent us high-quality color printing work, very expensive, and just the sort of thing that normally we loved to do. However, these jobs used to cause us a lot of problems and for a long time we could not work out why.

The printers hated them. As soon as the jobs got onto the press, everything seemed to go wrong. The colors changed constantly, so the ink levels had to be continually adjusted to compensate. The result was a lot of manual quality control afterwards in the bindery. We typically had to order more paper for these jobs so that we would have enough good copies to supply the quantity ordered. Also, given the additional time we spent getting the job done, we had to add around 15% to the price.

The problems eventually turned out to have been caused by the designers who created the digital files. They were using tint books to select very rich, dense colors that only used C, M, and Y. None of them contained any black at all. These color specifications were then applied to large solid areas in the job, as backgrounds to everything else.

As already mentioned, C, M, and Y are designed to be transparent, whereas black is designed to be opaque. When you are printing a transparent color onto white paper, the white of the paper becomes part of the color you see. When you print black, the paper does not show through, and so it is not involved with the color you see at all.

If, for example, you printed a 70% tint of magenta with a perfectly even flow of ink, all the sheets you printed would look the same. If the ink flow became lighter, so would the tint, simply because the ink is transparent. If there is not so much of it there, more of the paper is able to show through. Similarly, if the ink flow increases, the tint will get darker.

Running a press is a bit like driving a car. You cannot just set the steering wheel once and hope that you will keep following the road. You have to make constant adjustments—a little to the left, a little to the right —to get where you want to go. On the press, the operator has to increase the ink a little bit, then decrease, then increase—and so on—in order to maintain a balance between the ink flow coming down onto the plate and the amount that the paper takes away in the process of getting properly printed. So minor fluctuations are happening all the time.

When you have three transparent colors combining to create a tint, all present at fairly high percentages, then even minor fluctuations will mean that your tint changes color all the time.

This means that the operator will spend all day running up and down the press trying to make adjustments to each unit in turn to compensate. Not surprisingly, it is not much fun.

As an example, let us take a tint made up of 90% cyan, 70% magenta, and 60% yellow. Not only would it be quite difficult to print, it would also get through a lot of ink. This is definitely something to consider, because the colored inks are much more expensive than black.

However, most of the color can actually be removed from this mix and replaced with black.

Imagine drawing a horizontal line through the tint percentages at the highest possible point at which they are all present (which in this case would be 60%) and removing everything below it, leaving behind 30% cyan, 10% magenta and no yellow at all. Replace the ink we have removed (60%) with a 60% tint of black and we are getting close to having the same color (fig. **9.2**). Actually, in this case it would be rather light and would require further juggling to hit it exactly.

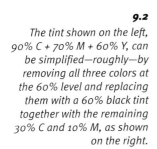

9.2

The tint shown on the left, 90% C + 70% M + 60% Y, can be simplified—roughly—by removing all three colors at the 60% level and replacing them with a 60% black tint together with the remaining 30% C and 10% M, as shown on the right.

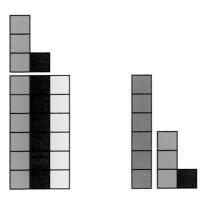

What we just did, of course, is to apply the theory behind GCR to remove most of the transparent colored inks from the tint. As a result, it is a lot easier to print because the bulk of the color is now carried by black —which, being opaque, is more stable even when there is some variation in the ink flow. And it is much cheaper.

It is easy enough to try this for yourself in Photoshop. Create a foreground CMYK color using just C, M, and Y, and then remove equal percentages of magenta and yellow and a slightly higher percentage of cyan. Then add the same percentage of black as you removed of magenta and yellow. You will have to juggle things further to get them to be the same, but it can always be done. The amazing thing is that Photoshop can do this automatically in images on a pixel-by-pixel basis.

The result of all this research was that we were able to substitute our own tints for those of the designers, and the printer was able to spend the day walking rather than running. The bindery was also happy because there was no more manual sheet-by-sheet quality control right through the job. But happiest of all was the client, when told that in future the price of his work would be 15% lower.

Highlights and mid-tones

Alas, the highlights still need watching. As with grayscale images, you can use "image/adjust/threshold" to find the lightest areas, and then place a marker there with the color-sampler tool (see chapter 7). If all four colors are present at less than 5%, then if you are printing on an average-quality coated stock (and of course, you should adjust this figure if you are using a different paper), none of them is likely to make it onto the final printed page. In that case, you will definitely need to adjust highlight levels to ensure that at least one of the colors will be present.

As for the mid-tones, you can use the same method as that used for grayscale images: backwards calibration (see chapter 6). Talk to your repro house, or whoever does your color scanning, and get hold of a selection of digital images together with their printed results. Make sure that the images they give you were not changed in any way before being included in the page-layout program and printed. Open them in Photoshop (and tell Photoshop to use the embedded profile, if it asks) and take a long, hard look, comparing the on-screen appearance with the printed materials. You should be able to tell immediately whether or not your monitor is telling you anything close to the truth. If it is not, try adjusting it for brightness, contrast and color. If your monitor does not have individual color adjustments, use "Adobe Gamma" (to find it on either PC or Mac, see chapter 6). However, if you do have individual color channel settings on your monitor, so much the better. Get the two images to look as close to each other as possible.

Once you know that you can more-or-less trust the overall picture you are seeing on screen, then you will know what kind of adjustments you need to make to your own work. If your monitor could not completely get to where you wanted to go, at least you should have gained an idea of what kind of image appearance on screen will produce what kind result in print.

A word of warning—it is very easy to overdo color changes, so be careful. If your image has even a few percentage points too many or too few of any of the colors, it will stand out as being too blue, green or whatever—especially if there are other images near it on the same page that are closer to a balanced range. These imbalances are known as **color casts**. To avoid missing these—and you would be surprised at just how easy that can be—I usually keep a few small images that I know are OK clearly visible on the screen while I am working with color adjustments, just for the comparison.

If there are no color casts in the image, and assuming you have by now taken care of the highlights, the only things remaining to fix are the mid-tones. You can make an adjustment to these using the "composite" channel (i.e. the one labelled "CMYK") in the "levels" window (fig. **9.3**). Grab the center arrow under the histogram and pull it either to the left or right. This will involve all the color channels together, making a balanced adjustment towards lighter or darker but without adding any particular hue.

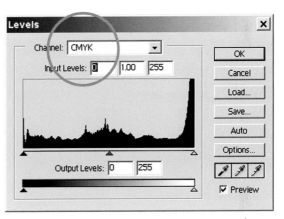

9.3

In this example, any adjustment made using the arrows underneath the histogram will affect all of the CMYK channels simultaneously.

Dealing with color balance

There are two kinds of color casts. One is caused by too much of a particular color and is fairly easy to figure out. These are "plus-color casts." The other is caused by too little of a particular color, and is much more difficult to pin down. These are "minus-color casts." Our inability to make a correct decision regarding this kind of image is usually caused by all the other things in our peripheral view muddying the visual waters. Reflections on the monitor screen are also common culprits. Nor will it work to see the image on its own, with nothing else getting in the way. What is needed are useful points of comparison.

If you are working with a plus-color cast then you might be able to make a simple adjustment to just one of the color channels. Here, color mode is important. For instance, if the plus-color was green, to adjust for it in CMYK mode would require changing the cyan as well as the yellow component.

As you can only do them one at a time, it would be difficult to get it right first time. However, if you change the mode to RGB you might be able to fix things with a single adjustment to the green channel.

Conversely, if a yellow adjustment is what is needed, working on the image in RGB mode would be quite difficult. You would be better off in CMYK mode.

If you want to adjust a particular channel without changing the others, go to levels and click on the arrow to the right of the channel name at the top of the window (fig. **9.4**). You can then select the one you want to work on. Moving the sliders or making numerical adjustments will then only affect the channel you have chosen. You can also use this method to adjust single channels in the "curves" window.

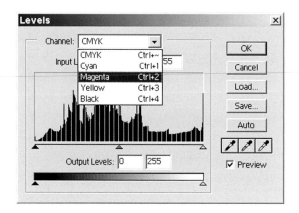

9.4
Selecting an individual color channel for adjustment using the "levels" window.

A very useful area for determining color balance is the "variations" window (fig. **9.5**). If you have not used variations before, this is what to do:

Open the image you want to adjust, and then choose "image/adjust/variations."

The variations window opens to show your original image in the top left corner. Beside it is one called "current pick." This is duplicated in the center of the array below and also at the center of the three images down the right-hand side.

The array gives you duplicate images with added R, G, and B as well as C, M, and Y, and the three on the right allow you to choose whether to lighten or darken it.

The idea is that when you click on one of the variations images, it becomes your current pick. You can click on as many choices as you want.

Finally clicking on "OK" accepts the changes you have made and updates your image in the main Photoshop window.

The advantages of variations lies mostly in its ability to show you changes caused by adding preset amounts of individual colors from either the RGB or CMYK systems. But what makes it truly useful is that it shows you how all of those adjustments would look simultaneously. So it gives you the points of comparison that you need in order to figure out what is wrong. You can compare how the original image looks against all the others and thus get a really good idea of the relative appearance.

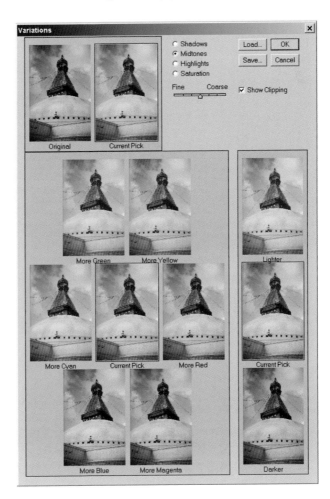

9.5

The "variations" window allows for the adjustment of any component of the RGB or CMYK color modes.

Despite thinking of variations as a wonderful tool, the adjustment levels of changes you can make here are limited to a handful of presets ranging from "coarse" to "fine." Therefore I do not consider it the best place to actually make adjustments, but I do use it to figure out which way things need to go. Then I adjust the appropriate channels in either levels or curves, which give a much wider range as well as greater sensitivity.

NOTE: Every time you go into the variations window, it is vital to remember to click on the image called "original" at the top left of the screen before you start making any decisions. This clears the settings made the last time you were there, which Photoshop will have remembered and already applied to the image array.

CHAPTER 10

Color-Management Systems

Photoshop color settings

You might wonder why this chapter is included at this point rather than before those dealing with grayscale and color calibration. The reason is simple. Many people will use the information presented in those chapters and find that they get along much better than they did before, but they still will not want to mess around with the color-management zone in Photoshop, which is a much more daunting prospect. This is an area that very few people understand, and if you do not understand it then you cannot really use it effectively. Most would rather just leave it alone and trust that the Photoshop defaults will not get them into too much trouble. While that is basically true, an overview of what this area can do for you is worthwhile, especially if it leads you towards actually making informed adjustments to your color settings at some time in the future.

However, please do not feel that you have to change your existing color settings if you do not want to. The defaults will work quite well for almost everything you do. The main thing is to pay attention to things like backwards calibration, highlights and shadows.

For those of you prepared to take the plunge, let us—briefly—get a little more complicated.

Certain conventions about color have been developed by a group called the International Color Consortium (ICC). Photoshop uses these conventions to determine its own color-management workflow. These are called "color-management systems" (CMS). The idea is to give appearance consistency to your images wherever they are displayed throughout the entire work process—all the way from your computer monitor right up to the pages rolling off the press. Otherwise, because there are many different CMYK "spaces" out there among print shops (caused by using different inks, for example) the results are unpredictable. A "CMYK color space" is the full range of colors that can be generated using all the possible combinations and tints of a particular set of CMYK pigments. An "RGB color space" holds all the RGB color combinations.

Similarly, while all monitors and scanners display and capture images using RGB, not all monitors and scanners share the same RGB space—aside from which most monitors are weak in terms of green and cyan display. So there are many variables, and making use of the Photoshop color settings is a way of overcoming the difficulties in consistency that might otherwise arise.

A CMS setting applies a color "profile" to an image which "tags" it with a description of how the colors included within it map to a particular color space. If you do not choose a profile, your image is "untagged," and instead picks up Photoshop's current working space profile as a default CMS. This then determines how your computer will display and edit the colors. If you choose a profile, it will be applied when, for example, you change the color mode of an image from RGB to CMYK. You can also choose whether or not to apply your resident settings to an image that is tagged with a different profile, as it is being opened.

If you already have an image open on screen, changing the profile settings will only affect the on-screen appearance. Actually tagging an image with the resident profile can only take place during the process of being opened.

As the settings have changed somewhat over the last few versions of Photoshop, I am including notes for versions 5 onwards. It does not make any difference whether you have a Mac or a PC.

Photoshop versions 5 and 5.5 both contain very similar color settings options. Versions 6, 7 and CS, while quite different from previous versions, are very also similar to each other. I am not going to deal with color settings in any versions earlier than 5 because I have to assume that anyone serious about graphic design will have updated since version 4, which, in terms of the computer industry, died out sometime between the Jurassic era and the present day.

I n both these versions, "color settings" can be found under the "file" menu. Selecting it displays choices for RGB, CMYK, Grayscale, and Profile set-up.

Photoshop 5 and 5.5

RGB set-up

For an RGB profile, choose "sRGB," which was designed for low-end printers (almost all the other settings were for video display) or "wide-gamut RGB" which tends to produce brighter, more saturated colors. You can use the "preview" button to see how the results may vary. "Wide-gamut" contains just about the entire visible spectrum, so it obviously contains many colors which cannot be printed.

Leaving "display using monitor compensation" checked does not change the information stored in the image but allows the monitor to give you a more accurate display.

CMYK set-up

For the "built-in" settings, versions 5 and 5.5 are the same. You can choose a profile from the drop-down list under "ink colors," according to the area in which you live. In the US, choose one of the "SWOP" settings. This actually stands for "specifications for web offset printing," but it is still probably your best bet. However, if you are actually running the job on a sheet-fed press, the dot-gain values might be quite different, typically about half the value you might expect from a web press. There is only one way to determine what the dot gain will actually be, and that is by asking your printer. If you can (and if there is time), get the printer to run a test for you using a calibration test strip as described in chapter 7. Once you know, you can enter the dot gain as a percentage value in the next section of the window. If you are in the UK, choose one of the "European" settings according to the kind of paper on which you are going to print.

For "separation type," make sure "GCR" is selected; "black ink limit" should be 100%, "total ink limit" should be 300%, and "UCA amount" should be 0%.

For the "ICC" settings, versions 5 and 5.5 are somewhat different. The options in version 5 are limited to the point that I do not recommend using any of them unless you have expert advice to the contrary. In version 5.5, however, several new profiles were added, including Euroscale coated and uncoated, and US web and sheet-fed options. As these sheet-fed profiles are not included in the "built-in" list, it is well worth selecting one of them, depending upon where you will print, and outputting for a sheet-fed operation. If you decide to do this, then choose "built-in" as your "engine" selection (this is not the same as choosing "built-in" from the top of the window) and "perceptual (images)" for the "intent."

Check the box next to "black point compensation," which will mean that the darkest neutral color of the incoming color space will be "mapped" to the darkest neutral color of the outgoing color space rather than to black. If you leave it unchecked, the darkest neutral color in your image will become black.

As "tables" offers only a single preset, I do not use it.

Grayscale set-up

You can either choose "black ink" or "RGB." If you select "black ink," then the same dot-gain values present in your current CMYK profile will be applied to grayscale images. If you choose "RGB," no dot-gain values will be applied. Whichever one you choose, it is still very important to fine-tune by "backwards calibration" (see chapter 6) after getting hold of printed samples.

Profile set-up

This area allows you to decide what to do with files that you have received from elsewhere that might have different profiles already assigned to them. If you choose "ask when opening" for all the options, you will be able to decide whether or not you want to convert them to your own settings.

You can save and load any settings you customize in this area.

Photoshop 6, 7, and CS

For these versions, "color settings" was moved to the "edit" menu. Instead of four separate choices, a single window opens which contains all the options together. When the cursor hovers over one of the settings shown, useful information about it appears in the "description" area.

In version 7 the options in the drop-down list opposite "settings" at the top of the window have been expanded to include US and European pre-press defaults. Select the one appropriate to where you happen to live. **NOTE:** If you choose the US defaults, you will actually be selecting values appropriate to web offset printing, including dot-gain compensation of at least 20%. If your work will be sent to a sheet-fed press, you will need to check the actual dot-gain compensation needed and customize the setting yourself. Similarly, the European settings use a dot-gain value more appropriate to sheet-fed output, so if you are actually printing on a web press, you will need to talk to the printer before customizing the dot-gain compensation value.

If this is the case, or if you are using version 6 (in which the "settings" options are fewer and do not include the US and European defaults), try the following.

Under "working spaces" is a list of four settings: the previously encountered RGB, CMYK, and grayscale settings and also a spot-color option, which was a new addition in version 6.

RGB set-up

For "RGB," choose Adobe RGB (1988) from the drop-down list. It is a wide-gamut space that is a good choice for eventual print-production work.

CMYK set-up

If you live in the US, pick one of the US coated or uncoated options for either sheet-fed or web printing.

If you are in Europe, choose "Euroscale coated v2" or "Euroscale uncoated v2," depending on the kind of paper you will be printing on. Both these choices are good for sheet-fed printing. If you intend to print on a web press, click on "custom CMYK" and select either the European coated or uncoated options and enter a custom dot-gain value according to information you can hopefully get from your printer. If your printer cannot tell you, for web try a value of 20%. Otherwise, as with the settings for versions 5 and 5.5, "separation type" should be "GCR"; "black ink limit" should be 100%; "total ink limit" should be 300%; and "UCA amount" should be 0%.

Incidentally, it is interesting to note that the "US prepress defaults" and "Europe prepress defaults" options available in Photoshop 7+ appear to assume that if you are in the US you are printing on a web, but if you live in Europe you are printing on a sheet-fed machine.

Grayscale set-up

For "grayscale," the "gray gamma 2.2" setting is the default gamma setting for Windows computers. Mac users will want to choose "gray gamma 1.8" instead. This setting is primarily used for online or video work and does not actually compensate for dot gain. It therefore allows the "backwards calibration" method to work for you regardless of the kind of paper you are printing on.

Spot colors

For "spot" dot-gain compensation, you should again enter a figure which is based on information you should be able to get from your printer. This will again vary considerably depending on the kind of machine and the kind of paper that you are printing on. If you use several different print shops, you might end up with a custom "spot" setting for each.

Other settings

Under "color management policies" in the central section of the window there are three conversion settings and three profile settings.

For "RGB," choose "convert to working RGB."

For "CMYK," choose "convert to working CMYK."

For "gray," choose "convert to working gray."

Then check all three of the "profile" boxes.

These conversion settings mean that whenever you open an image to which another profile—or even no profile at all—has been attached, Photoshop will convert them to your chosen profiles. And, by checking the three "profile" boxes, you ensure that you get another chance to change your mind before any such conversion occurs, even when you are pasting areas between images with mismatched profiles.

Now go back up and check the small box called "advanced mode" at the top left corner of the "color settings" window. This opens up another small section below "color management policies" called "conversion options."

For "engine," select "Adobe ACE."

For "intent," select "perceptual."

The Adobe ACE engine is best for RGB to CMYK conversion, while "perceptual" rendering compresses the RGB space into the target space. This means it retains the balance of the original, and that makes it particularly suitable for photographic images.

Underneath those two settings, "use black point compensation" should remain checked, as should "use dither." "Black point compensation" maps the darkest color of the source image to the darkest color of the destination color space, while "dithering" will help to prevent image banding—whether it is on screen or in the final print.

In the "advanced controls" area, leave both "desaturate monitor colors by" and "blend RGB colors using gamma" unchecked. The first, a percentage setting, is very likely to cause the on-screen appearance to be further away from the printed result and is recommended for expert use only. The second applies a specific gamma setting and is not a method most other applications will recognize.

Then click on "save" and give your custom settings a name and a description. The description will then appear in the box at the foot of the window whenever that setting is chosen.

Even though I believe that using the above settings will help to improve the quality of image output, if you have any serious doubts then please do not feel that everything will turn to garbage if you simply leave things as they are. It is OK to go slowly. Do not feel that you have to change any of your settings, yet. Talk to your printer, who may be able to help you decide; if not, you could also try a technical support call to Adobe. The chances are you will still feel unsure, because this is stuff you are unlikely to have heard much about, even if you have just completed your degree. If you would like to try making some basic changes but also want to tread carefully, then, if you live in the US, pick a coated or uncoated option for either sheet-fed or web and leave it at that. Similarly, if you live in the UK, simply pick one of the European defaults for your CMYK setting and do not change anything else. The sky will not fall on your head, and you will soon have added to your experience to the point that you will probably feel confident about going a little further.

Calibration test-strip settings

In chapter 7 I suggested creating a calibration test strip to help you figure out highlight, shadows and dot-gain levels. If you decide to make one of these in Illustrator or CorelDraw and then open it in Photoshop to see if the tint values are accurate, you should be aware that some of the choices you will be offered as you open it could affect the tint values shown. These notes are intended to help you decide what to do.

Photoshop always checks to see whether the image you are trying to open already has an applied color profile. If it has not, or if the assigned profile is different from the one you are currently using, you will get one or more message windows appearing prior to the file actually opening on-screen. Depending on the choice you make at this point, the tint values in the image will either stay as they are or change.

Generally, for images that you wish to work on in Photoshop, this is not a problem. If you are using a particular CMS in Photoshop, and have subsequently applied backwards calibration to your monitor settings, then the combination of the two is already taking care of dot gain in a satisfactory way. But in the case of a calibration test strip, it is important that none of the tint values change at all, and so in this case the CMS must not be allowed to get in the way.

First, do not let the source program in which you create the strip attach a color profile to it. If you are going to use Adobe Illustrator, go to "edit/color settings" and choose "color management off" from the drop-down "settings" list. If you are using CorelDraw, when you export the file as a TIFF, make sure that the "use color profile" box is not selected (for more about the TIFF file format, see chapter 11). Then, when you open the resulting file in Photoshop, choose the "leave as-is" option.

If, for example, you instead picked "dot gain 10%," the tint values will undergo major changes. The calibration test-strip tint values between 0–10% will become 0–6%. The 50% tint becomes 34%, and the 91–100% tints become 76–100%.

However, if you choose the "leave as is" option and then re-save the file as a TIFF image, if you open it up again you will see another window telling you that the "document has an embedded profile that does not match the current gray working space" box. Of the three choices it then offers, "use the embedded profile [instead of the working space]" will result in no change to the original tints; "convert document's colors to the working space" results in the same kind of changes already noted above; and "discard the embedded profile [do not color manage]" also leaves the tints unchanged.

CHAPTER 11

Good and Bad Image Formats

Good image formats

Here we take a look at the different kinds of images commonly available to a graphic designer with a view to figuring out which ones are OK to use and which ones are best to ignore. We will start with the good ones.

As far as offset printing is concerned, there are only two image formats that you ever want to end up with. First are TIFF files, second are various kinds of EPS. And that is all. Forget JPEG, GIF, PNG, BMP, PSD, everything. That is not to say that the image cannot be one of those formats at some point. It is just not something you want to end up with.

TIFF (tagged image file format)

TIFF (shortened to "TIF", on a PC) files can be simple bitmaps (two-color images in which each pixel can be just one of the colors), grayscale images, RGB or CMYK. The important thing about them is that each pixel is allowed to be anything it wants to be within the given range of the image and the applied color profile. As uncompressed images, they tend to be quite large; a full-bleed A4 CMYK TIFF at 300 dpi can be anything between 30 to 40 megabytes. In Photoshop there is a **lossless** (i.e. no loss of quality) compression option for TIFF files called LZW (Lemple-Zif-Welch), and while it saves on disk space it can sometimes cause problems for the printer, so do not use TIFF files in a page layout that have the compression option still attached. Open them and re-save, turning the "LZW" button off during the process. I avoid this option in general because several times now I have saved something as TIFF using LZW only to end up with a corrupted image that cannot be opened at all.

Although it is possible to save a multi-layer image in TIFF format, it may lead to problems if it is placed into a page layout. Therefore I almost always save multi-layered files in Photoshop format (PSD), and only "flattened" (i.e. single layer) images as TIFF files. The only exception to this rule is when I intend to place text on top of an image in Photoshop, but only if I am using version 6 or later. In that case I can save the text as vector information on a separate layer as part of a TIFF file. This means that when the result is placed into a page layout, the text will be able to print out at the maximum resolution of a postscript printer rather than being held to the same resolution as the image. This is particularly useful when the text involved is small. However, if it is above 40 pt I usually flatten the text layer into the background.

Otherwise, TIFF files are generally simple. They do not even need a postscript printer to output them. The data just gets processed, one pixel at a time, until the whole thing is done. I cannot remember ever having a problem with a TIFF. Problems are always caused by something else.

EPS (encapsulated PostScript)

EPS files are very, very useful, but I do not agree with people who tell me that EPS is the preferred image format for everything. They definitely have their uses, but there are also some disadvantages.

EPS files can be one of two basic kinds: "vector" or "bitmap." Bit-mapped EPS files are like TIFFs in that they are resolution-dependent, i.e. they have a fixed resolution based on the number of pixels there are to the inch. The amount of detail they can display is limited to the detail captured during their creation, whether it was by scanner, digital camera or Photoshop. Increasing the resolution later merely spreads the original data over more pixels. This might smooth the pixelated edges somewhat, but it does not add any detail beyond what was there to begin with.

However, if you have drawn an object in Adobe Illustrator and saved it as an EPS file, or drawn the same thing in CorelDraw and exported it as an Adobe Illustrator or EPS file, then it is a vector image and not a bitmap. This means it is not resolution-dependent and can instead be infinitely scaled to any size. Even if the image was drawn on a tiny section of the page, it can be enlarged to fit on the side of a bus—and it would look as sharp and clean as if you had zoomed in to view the original. Better still, both these formats support a transparent background, so you can import them into a page layout and place them on top of an existing background with no problem.

EPS files of this kind are also quite small—and it can be a bit of a shock to discover that the logo which you have created and which will soon be screen-printed, 3 meters tall, onto the side of a supermarket truck is only 18kb in size.

Other things you should know about EPS files

There are, as I mentioned, some disadvantages with EPS files.

None of the major page-layout programs—Quark, PageMaker, and

InDesign—can actually show you a real EPS image. All they can do is display the **image header**, i.e. a low(er)-resolution TIFF that lies on top of the PostScript code so that you can at least see where the image has been placed, and roughly how it looks. I say roughly because the maximum depth for an image header is usually 8-bit, so it can only show you 256 colors—much like a GIF. This means that what you have to look at while you are working has a quality level which is less than superb. The true, high-quality image beneath it only appears when it is ripped ("raster image processed"—turning the vector information of the EPS file into halftone dots) with a PostScript printer.

Personally, I prefer to work with high-resolution images on screen whatever program I am working in. It just helps the creative flow. If I am constantly having to deal with lower image quality on screen while I am trying to design something, then things just tend not to flow as well as they otherwise might.

Clipping path problems

Another problem with EPS files is that sometimes they will not print, especially if there is a **clipping path** involved.

Just in case you have not run into these, a clipping path is an outline drawn on an image which acts as a mask. When the image is placed in the page-layout program, nothing outside the outline can appear. Clipping paths are usually created either in Photoshop or in the page-layout program being used for final document assembly. You will find details on how to create a clipping path later in this chapter.

If a clipping path has too many **nodes** in it (i.e. points which anchor the path into a particular shape), the PostScript code involved can overload the printer and the result is... no result at all. Imagine you have put together a 64-page magazine filled with EPS files, many with clipping paths, and you decide to run a final proof copy to send out with the file. The little light on the laser printer flashes for a while, keeps flashing, goes on flashing, nothing coming out and finally it quits, probably while you are not looking. What happened? Nine times out of ten, it will be an EPS file that happened—or, rather, that did *not* happen. The trouble is, you now have to go back through the document, deleting them one at a time, and then once again attempting to print that page. It might take hours—even days—to find the problem file. This is definitely something to avoid!

You can apply clipping paths to vector or bitmap images, but there are other ways of dealing with them that will avoid most of the problems. For me, that immediately relegates clipping paths to the "I really do not want to have to use these" box. However, if you insist on giving yourself those nail-biting moments, consider the following.

Vector images

There is no need to add clipping paths to files saved in Adobe Illustrator (.ai) format. It is much easier simply to open them up in Illustrator or import them into CorelDraw, remove any unwanted background, and re-save them again in the same format. Vector images saved in Encapsulated PostScript (.EPS) format, however, might pose some problems. Even though you can import them into Illustrator or CorelDraw, you cannot actually do anything with them in either program other than re-size them on the page. In this case, there is no alternative but to open them in Photoshop in order to deal with unwanted background areas. Doing so immediately makes them resolution-dependent, which unfortunately negates their main advantage, i.e. infinite scaleability. In fact, when you try to open an EPS image, Photoshop will immediately ask for the size and resolution at which you want it to be opened. When you enter your requirements and click OK, the EPS information gets rasterized into pixels at the resolution you have specified. If your vector image contains fine outlines that are made up of color tints, these will get rasterized into dots, too, which will probably make them look fuzzy.

Bitmap images

These can be opened in Photoshop where you can create a clipping path on them quite easily. An example of when you might be tempted to use a clipping path on a bitmapped image might be, for instance, when you have a logo on a colored background—and you need to get rid of the background because the logo has to overlap an area of a different color which has already been created in the page layout.

The main thing to consider from the point of view of appearance is that any clipping path you create on a bitmap image is actually a vector outline. It will completely disregard the shape of the pixels in whatever bitmap it is applied to and march right across them. This means that an **anti-aliased** edge is impossible, and the result is quite likely to look as if it has been cut out and pasted into place. (Anti-aliasing is a slight falling-off of tone around the edge of an element which gives it a slightly soft edge and enables it to blend in visually with the rest of the image much more than would otherwise be possible. It is also applied to items such as menu text on your computer screen, thus allowing it to have a smooth appearance despite being part of a comparatively low-resolution display.)

Sometimes that sharp-edged look might be what you want. But if not, you can use Photoshop to re-create the color background that is in the page-layout program. Then import the logo, flatten the layers, and save the whole thing as a TIFF. The result will not look as if it was cut out and pasted on, and it will definitely print.

This method does mean doing some careful measuring to make sure that the logo actually ends up in the right place, but it is easy to check that. Generate a duplicate file of background and logo, flatten it, bump the resolution down to 72 dpi and save as a reasonably good-quality RGB JPEG. Then you can import it and see if the placement is going to work.

Although it might seem tedious, if you get into the habit of looking ahead, then you probably will not have bothered to create the shape in the page-layout program in the first place. Instead you will have already done it in Photoshop. But these things take time. Expect to do it the long way around a few times before you get into the habit.

If you decide instead to continue with a clipping path/bitmap EPS combination, remember that you will end up with a file that none of the page-layout programs can actually show you. Instead, you will be looking at the 256-color **image header** file in its place.

If that is OK with you, then go for it. But remember to try printing it on a PostScript printer as soon as possible after placing it on the page. If it prints on your own PostScript printer, it should also print without any problems on an imagesetter.

Creating a clipping path

While I do not much care for clipping paths and almost never use them, I could not, in good conscience, let this book go out without offering some help to those of you who might want to use them but are unfamiliar with the process. Here is a method using Photoshop, which is the best program to use because of its ability to create selections which can then be turned into paths.

For an example, fig. **11.1** shows a small TIFF image showing a green ball on a shaded background. Let us assume you wanted to place the ball, without the background, on top of a blue bar that you have already created in the page-layout document.

In order to create a clipping path around the ball, you could use one of several of the selection tools in Photoshop. In my example I have simply drawn a circular selection.

11.1
The source file for the clipping path examples shown in fig. 11.2.

To actually turn the selection into a path, you now have two choices.

First, if you go to the options arrow at the top right of the "paths" window in Photoshop and then select "make work path," you get the chance to enter a tolerance factor. The tightest tolerance available is 0.5 pixels, and this will create a path which will be the closest possible to your original selection. An entry of 1.0 will make it slightly looser, and so on up to 10, which will be very loose (see fig. **11.2**).

11.2
On the left, the green ball has a clipping path applied with a tolerance of 0.5 pixels. The ball in the center is the same but with a tolerance of 1 pixel. The background element for both these has been created in the page-layout program. Right, a composite image of the same elements created as a TIFF file in Photoshop.

Alternatively, if you click on the "make work path from selection" button at the foot of the paths window, Photoshop will remember the same tolerance factor chosen the last time a work path was created and apply that without giving you further options.

NOTE: Each point at which the path suddenly changes direction involves a node which anchors it in place, so if you choose 0.5 as your tolerance factor you could be creating an object that is too complex to print. A setting of 1.0 smooths things out without losing the overall shape of your selection, and this is usually a better choice.

Duotones, DCS, and PDF files

There are three other kinds of EPS files that are impossible to avoid and which deserve a special mention: a) **Duotones**, which are two-color images, typically made up of black plus a Pantone color (Pantone colors are discussed in chapter 15) b) DCS (desktop color separation files) and c) PDF files.

Duotones

Duotones, alas, tend to be calibrated poorly or not at all, resulting in a muddy appearance in the mid-tones. This usually happens because both the color channels in the image have been left with the same spread of emphasis. If you "bend" the mid-tone region of the lighter color to make it somewhat brighter (fig. **11.3**), this problem can be avoided. This is very much like making an adjustment using "curves." Go into the duotone adjustment area ("image/mode/duotone") and click on the square with the diagonal line crossing it (this appears to the left of the square containing your color choice in the duotone window). If needed, the black channel can also be adjusted using the same method.

11.3

By clicking on the square showing the diagonal slash next to "Ink 2" in the "duotone options" window, the "duotone curve" window is opened. The line can be pulled into a new shape in a very similar way to the "curves" window, thus influencing the spread of tone within the image. Pulling it down in the center will reduce the mid-tone strength of the selected color.

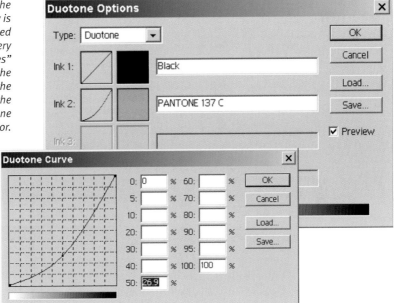

Duotones containing spot (Pantone) colors can be included as part of a composite, rather than a separated PDF document when Distiller is used as the printer. If you are in doubt as to whether the spot colors made the transition, place the resulting PDF file into a new Quark, PageMaker or InDesign document, and then click on "file/print." If you select a PostScript printer, the correct Pantone colors should show up as additional color-separation options.

If you want to use a duotone as part of a CMYK print run, then do not leave it in its two-color EPS format, or you will be adding the Pantone to the job as a fifth color—and therefore also adding a lot of additional expense. Instead, convert the duotone image into CMYK format and save it as a TIFF. It will look pretty much the same, so long as you calibrate it reasonably well.

DCS (desktop color separations)

Desktop Color Separations are another form of EPS file that are sometimes unavoidable, but which can be very useful. There are two formats: DCS1 and DCS2.

DCS1 images are made up of five separate files: the four individual elements of the color separation plus a preview composite. I do not use DCS1 files at all as they are just a pain to print. Instead, I convert any such files into TIFF (or occasionally EPS) format and use that instead.

DCS2 format supports spot channel colors in addition to the four-color separation and preview and can be saved either in a multi-file format or as a single composite image.

These are seriously useful when the need for them arises. If you have to add a spot (Pantone) color to a CMYK image, DCS2 is the only format that can do it. For an in-depth discussion of the use of Pantone colors and the DCS2 format, see "Typical scenario 3" in chapter 15.

PDF (portable document format)

Anything saved as a PDF file using Adobe Acrobat's Distiller or PDF Writer can be placed into PageMaker, InDesign, or QuarkXPress 5+ (but not Quark 4; to do that, you have to open the file in Illustrator and then save it again in EPS format). After all, a PDF file is an image captured in a PostScript format, and therefore very similar to EPS and DCS files. And, just like EPS and DCS files, there is usually nothing much you can do to edit it once it has been created and saved. If the file from which it was generated contained mistakes, well, you get everything: warts and all. This means that a PDF file can end up containing RGB colors, seriously compressed images, no trapping, and sometimes the fonts will have been embedded and sometimes not. Also, while a PDF file might contain many pages, only one page can be selected for display if it is imported into a page layout program.

The good news is that PDF files, just like true EPS files, can contain both vector and bitmapped images. This makes them incredibly versatile and useful—especially if you want to send your printer a high-resolution file that needs nothing else done to it prior to film or plate output. See chapter 17 for more information about creating PDF files.

You can also open a single-page PDF file, or one page of a multiple-page PDF file, in Photoshop. But remember that if you do this, as it is an EPS file, the whole thing will first be converted into a bitmap, including type and vector information.

Bad image formats

At this point I should mention that most of the "bad" file formats will actually print quite well on a desktop systems but nevertheless cannot be included in files sent out for offset printing. The main reason for this is that desktop printers, both laser and inkjet, are built to print RGB images and not CMYK. However, higher-level systems such as imagesetters are built to deal very well with CMYK but not with RGB.

To further confuse us, most of the page-layout programs display a very reasonable on-screen view of an RGB image, whereas CMYK images often look very odd indeed. Because of this, it is extremely important to check that you are not only using the correct kind of image but also to make absolutely sure it is in CMYK format before sending it out.

GIF (graphics interchange format)

GIF is a great format for web sites, especially for images that can be made up of a small number of colors and/or large areas of flat color— maps, for example, or single-color text headings with a drop shadow applied. Do not use the GIF format for images with lots of color graduations such as continuous-tone images. This is the more regular "photo" type of image, and although they can be saved in GIF format easily enough, you will end up with much bigger files than if you had saved them as a JPEG.

GIF files are in **indexed color** format, which means they can display a maximum of 256 colors—and that is it. However, they can be *any* 256 colors. For example, when you save an image with perhaps several thousand different colors in GIF format, the 256 commonest colors in the original will become the entire palette. If more colors are needed to give a closer approximation to the original, GIF files can dither them together —which means a scattering of one of the colors is thrown in among the pixels of another, creating an illusion of a blend of the two when looked at from a distance. Dithering is a very memory-intensive way of producing additional colors and using it will usually produce a considerably larger file size.

ImageReady, the web software bundled with Photoshop from versions 5.5 onwards, can show you all 256 colors currently existing in your GIF file. It also enables you to select colors and delete them one at a time to see if the image suddenly degrades beyond what you are happy with. This means you can end up with as few colors as you can possibly get away with. If you can get away with 8, 16, 32, or even 64 colors in your image then there is a very good chance that you will end up with a substantially smaller file size than if you saved the same thing in JPEG format.

Sometimes it is possible to change a GIF into a reasonably good TIFF which can be used in a four-color print run. It either has to be a large enough image to make a successful conversion into a TIFF, or you need to be using it considerably smaller than its original size. The results have a tendency to look grainy because of the limitations on the number of colors imposed by the GIF format. If in doubt, convert a copy to an RGB TIFF and try printing it on a high-resolution inkjet machine (i.e. an inkjet which can print at a resolution of at least 720 dpi) to get some idea of how it might look in print.

JPEG (joint photographic experts group)

JPEGs, (shortened to "JPG" on a PC, as a maximum of three letters are allowed for the file extension) like TIFFs, can utilize a range of up to 16.7 million colors in RGB format and 4.5 billion in CMYK. However, unlike TIFFs, JPEG is a **lossy** format, which means that, at whatever quality level you choose to save it, you are losing information that you will never get back. Each time the image is re-saved, you lose a little more. At a high quality level, it is not a huge problem. At a low level, it is horrible.

If you save a file as a JPEG you have the option of selecting, in Photoshop 6, for example, any one of thirteen quality levels (0 to 12, 0 being the lowest). To see for yourself what a lossy form of compression can do to an image, try the following.

Crop a small section from an image. Try to select something with a range of "busy" detail and smooth detail—the skyline area of a building is ideal, as shown in fig. **11.4**. Make a duplicate, and then save one at a high quality level (10 or more), and the other at zero quality level.

You will probably have to close the low-quality version and re-open it in order to see the changes. Even then, you may not see a great deal of difference between the two images until you zoom in. Then the differences are obvious.

Saving as a JPEG—at any quality level—divides the image into squares, each measuring 8 pixels on a side. An **algorithm** (a pattern, basically) is applied to each of these squares. The higher the quality level, the more complex the algorithm. If it has been saved at level 10 or higher (the possible range will vary depending upon which version of Photoshop you are using) and then resaved as a TIFF file for printing, very few people would be able to tell from the final printed image—especially without the original to compare it to—that it was ever saved as a JPEG. At level 0, it is another matter altogether. The "pattern" at this level is so simple that there is only vague detail left in any of the squares. Also, because of this simplicity, you can end up with a pinkish square next to a greenish square, next to a bluish square—it is as if each becomes a completely separate mini-image that takes little or no notice of its surroundings. Where a square overlaps both a detailed area and a flat area, the flat area gets disturbed because the turbulence of the detail affects the whole pattern. The result is called **artifacting**, and it makes it look as if every object in the image is generating a heat haze.

11.4

On the left, the image has been saved as a level-10 JPEG on a scale of 0-12. On the right, at level 0. Both have been enlarged so that the pixels are visible.

There is really never going to be a good reason for saving an image as a medium- to low-quality level JPEG. If you need a smaller file size, use **optimization** instead (see chapter 12). Otherwise, save at the highest quality level possible.

Incidentally, when saving a JPEG, only choose one of the "progressive" settings if you are saving it for web-site display. This allows an image to load on screen at very low resolution quite quickly, then gradually update itself to the complete image in either two, three or four more passes. Therefore its only purpose is to give viewers something to look at in an attempt to prevent them from getting bored and deciding to go to a different web site instead. The progressive setting has no place in the world of print.

Almost all the other formats

I am not going to detail all the various names, benefits and uses of other image formats because this book is primarily concerned with printing questions. The Internet is now such a feature of our lives that GIFs and JPEGs are extremely common, and I am constantly running into problems arising from their use as printed images. I have therefore included those specifically in this chapter, whereas other file formats are less common. If you run into one of them, zoom in and take a long and close look at the quality of detail before you decide to use it, but convert them to either TIFF or one of the EPS formats before doing so—and make sure they are *all* CMYK!

12

Using Images from the Web

Optimization and resolution

It is really not a good idea to just download whatever you like from the web and use it. If you do, you may find yourself on the receiving end of a lawsuit. Before going ahead, make sure you have permission from the owner of the copyright. Otherwise it could be a very costly mistake.

Assuming you have received the go-ahead, you should also use the opportunity to request a better copy of the image you want to use. Otherwise, what you are left with is only very rarely going to be suitable for printing. This is for several reasons: web images are always RGB; they are almost always JPEG or GIF format; and their resolution is 72 dpi—much too low to be of use unless you shrink the image to a smaller physical size in order to increase resolution. Besides that, if it is a JPEG it has probably been optimized.

Optimization

Optimization is not yet a universal practice, so you might be lucky enough to find that the image you want to use is actually fairly high-quality. If not, an optimized image is a better starting point than if someone has tried to decrease the file size merely by saving the JPEG at a lower quality level. When that happens, the image is seriously damaged. Optimization, on the other hand, decreases the file size by a much greater amount, but—oddly enough—leaves the image appearance much closer to the original.

Think of it like this: your image has a surface, which you can see, and a depth, which you cannot see. If you save at lower and lower quality levels, you are removing detail from the surface and leaving distortion ("artifacting") in its place. If you optimize it instead, you are whittling away at the unseen depths and leaving the surface more-or-less undisturbed.

As an example, let us take the image that I already used to demonstrate the effects of JPEG compression in chapter 11. Clearly, the image saved at quality level 10 was far superior to the one saved at level 0—and yet in terms of file size, the level 10 image was 13 kb, and the level 0 image was only 11 kb. Not a huge difference—certainly not a very useful difference. The optimized image, on the other hand, was 3 kb, and not visibly different. I have re-saved it as a TIFF file in order to be able to print it, and here it is next to the original (fig. **12.1**). Can you tell which is which?

Obviously, if you have to use a web image, you are going to be in much better shape if you can use an image that has been carefully optimized rather than one that has been damaged through being saved at a low-quality level.

12.1
The one on the right is the optimized image.

How to optimize an image

There are no good reasons for optimizing an image if you intend to subsequently place it into a page layout for print. However, when you need to send a good-quality on-screen proof to someone as an e-mail attachment, it can be useful.

After you have saved the high-resolution image as a TIFF or EPS file in Photoshop, but while the image is still open on screen, choose "file/ save for web." On the window which then opens, the image will appear on the left, and the options on the right. Above the image are some tabs. Click on "2-up." This produces a duplicate image to the right of the original. At the foot of each image is information telling you the current format and file size. The copy also displays the download time at a particular modem speed.

In the "settings" section on the right, choose "JPEG" as the file format. Underneath that are four quality-level presets, and you can use the percentage slider to the right to fine-tune between them. As you make adjustments to the quality settings, the file size and download time are re-calculated and the information below the copy image updates. At the same time, the result of the new settings is applied to the copy, which you can therefore compare to the unchanged original next to it. When you are happy with both the file size and the appearance of the copy, choose "save." You will be then prompted for a name and a location for the new file.

Resolution

Before discussing the specifics relating to the resolution problems with web images, it would probably be useful to detail briefly the different kinds of resolution terminology that designers encounter.

Let us start with your computer screen. It (usually) has a fixed resolution of 72 dpi if it is a Mac, and 96 dpi if it is a PC. That "dpi" refers to the viewing resolution only, and is the reason images placed on web sites need a resolution of 72 dpi, which is the lowest common denominator between the two systems.

If you have assembled a page layout comprising 300 dpi images—i.e. 300 pixels-per-inch images—and vector text, your screen can show you nothing better than a 72 or 96 dpi screen image, though of course you can view the page at different levels of detail by using the "zoom" controls.

If you print the same page on a laser printer, it is most likely generating a 600 dpi print. That means that the blobs of toner it lays down are approximately $1/600$ of an inch across. This figure has nothing to do with the resolution of the elements you have placed on your page. It merely limits the detail possible in the print.

Similarly, inkjet machines typically print at resolutions of 1440 dpi or greater. This refers to the size of the tiny droplets of ink that they spray out in order to create the print, and again has nothing whatsoever to do with the digital resolution of the images and text being printed.

Finally, the imagesetter which produces either the final film or plates from which the job will be offset-printed might have a resolution of 2400 dpi or greater. This allows it to generate variable dot sizes within the halftones it makes from the 300 dpi images in the page layout. The resolution of these halftones is described as either **lpi** (lines per inch) or a "line screen," which refers to how many of rows of halftone dots there are to the linear inch.

All web images are saved at 72 dpi, and you probably want them at 300 dpi at the size they are required to print (for more about optimum scanning values, see chapter 13).

If you have a downloaded image that is 4 in (100 mm) wide, and you want to print at 2 in (50 mm) wide, it is easy to think that you have already got roughly half the resolution you need—because 72 dpi over a width of 4 in (100 mm) requires the same number of pixels (283 of them) as 144 dpi over a width of 2 in (50 mm), and 144 is roughly half of 300. (Digital images are generally believed by graphic designers to need a resolution of at least 300 dpi in order to print using offset litho. This is not quite accurate, but good enough for now. See chapter 13 for more detailed information.)

Actually, that is the view of the optimist. As an example, let us take an image that measures exactly one inch by one inch. If its resolution is 72 dpi, how close are we to what we really need if we want to print it at that size using offset litho?

Seventy-two dpi means 72 pixels for each vertical and horizontal inch of image dimension. That is a total of 72 x 72, or 5,184 pixels per square inch. At 300 dpi, it is 300 x 300. That is 90,000, which is 17.361 times as many pixels. That means your original contains slightly less than 1/17 of the detail you would have if you had been able to start out with an optimum-resolution scan instead.

Small wonder that very few web images are worth more than a cursory glance when they are needed for offset printing.

However—what about if your image could actually be fairly convincingly enlarged to, say, 150 dpi? In other words, a method that does a better job than merely spreading the original information over a larger number of pixels?

I have successfully taken images that, at first, seemed completely impossible to work with and ended up with images that not only printed without pixelation or color casts, but were very convincing. It does not work all the time, but even having it work once can make it worthwhile.

Genuine Fractals Print Pro

There are several programs available that can do a better job of enlarging images than Photoshop, and if you often need to do that kind of work you should definitely consider getting hold of one of them. For the following example I used one called *Genuine Fractals Print Pro* (made by the Altimira Group) which acts as a Photoshop plug-in and is available on both PC and Mac platforms. Due to its long name I am just going to refer to it as "GFPP" from now on. It allows you to save an image in a proprietary format (which gives it an ".stn" extension on a PC) either in a lossless or almost lossless condition.

As your web image will not bear any more loss than it has already been subjected to, let us assume you would want to save it in lossless format. When you re-open it, you can specify a resolution and size that are considerably larger than the original and end up with a much better result than if you merely went to "image/image size" in Photoshop and increased the pixel count. GFPP manages to keep the detail much sharper as it increases the image, which actually gives the appearance of detail where none existed before. For instance, if there is an object with a curved edge somewhere in the image, merely increasing the pixel count means you end up with a bigger, softer-looking curve. GFPP increases the pixel count while allowing the curve to stay sharp. That means you end up with a picture that is clearer and sharper as well as bigger—maybe even big enough to print.

12.2

The original image (left) and copies enlarged using Photoshop (center) and GFPP (right).

Fig. **12.2** shows: left, the original 72 dpi web capture; center, a copy which has been held to the same dimensions but in which the resolution has been increased to 300 dpi using "image/image size" in Photoshop (this method is called "interpolation," and it means that the original information has simply been spread over a larger number of pixels); and right, another copy which has also been held to the same dimensions, but saved using GFPP and then re-opened at 300 dpi.

Let us take a look at a slice of each of them, in the same order as shown in 12.2, but stretched to a much larger size (fig. **12.3**).

12.3

The same three images as in 12.2, enlarged to show detail.

See how the edges are more clearly defined on the right-hand image. Also, note how much cleaner and smoother this image looks compared to the lumpiness of the interpolated image in the center.

Of course, lack of resolution is not the only thing getting in the way when you want to use a JPEG downloaded from the web. In almost every case, there will be severe artifacting due to the lower quality level at which it has been saved. Just about the only way to get rid of some of it is to use the "clone stamp" tool in Photoshop. The main problem areas will be areas such as skies, where detail from the horizon will have influenced the 8 x 8 pixel blocks that overlap the much lighter and smoother areas of sky above them. This interference will have been improved somewhat during the interpolation process, but now it will have to be dealt with.

You might think that it is better to deal with these areas before making them even bigger. However, even though these areas are larger after being re-sized using the method above, it is usually preferable to make repairs with the cloning tool *after* enlargement rather than while it is a 72-dpi image. Higher resolution gives you more room to move around, and a smoother subject from which to clone better-quality tone.

The key to successful cloning is to redefine continually your source point. I cannot stress this enough. If you do not, you will see repetition patterns here and there, or simply areas that do not look right because the detail in them does not match the surrounding area.

Using GIF images

This can be very difficult because, as mentioned in chapter 11, the GIF format only allows 256 different colors to appear in the image. Therefore, in order to create the illusion of an image with a much more extensive palette, a GIF has to scatter pixels of one of the existing colors in among the pixels of another. Then there is a good chance that our eyes will think they are seeing all the shades between the two that do not really exist.

Sometimes a GIF will have been optimized to hold less than 256 colors, and this of course only tends to make things worse.

All that can be done is to convert the image back into either RGB or CMYK mode, and then increase the image size by at least 10%. This allows the creation of new pixels that can "choose" their color from the entire range available in the color space you have selected.

Unfortunately, due to the small physical dimensions of most web-based GIF images, it is unlikely that you will end up with something that you are very happy with in print. The only bright spot on this particular horizon is that more complex images (i.e. photographs rather than created graphics) are much more likely to have been saved as a JPEG than as a GIF, and that gives you a better chance of ending up with something that you might be able to use.

CHAPTER 13

Scanning

Scanning original material

Most designers I have talked to about scanning have been told that they are supposed to scan everything at 300 dpi, but they do not really know why. In fact, there is a formula that can be applied to any scanning project which shows that 300 dpi is not, in fact, the magic number for all scans, all the time.

There are two factors involved in determining how much of the original detail a scanned image can hold. One is the dpi, which determines how many pixels there are per inch of scanned image. The other is the percentage of enlargement or reduction at which the original has been scanned. If you only have one of these pieces of information then, excuse the pun, you do not have the whole picture.

For example, I am often asked to send images here and there, and told that they are needed at something like "roughly 10 x 12 inches." As I explained in chapter 12, the file size of a 10 x 12 inch image at 72 dpi is very different from a 10 x 12 inch image at 300 dpi. Unless I am told the resolution as well as the size, I have no way of knowing exactly what is required. Sometimes Photoshop is not available to the person receiving the images, so if I send something that is seventeen times bigger than needed—and perhaps in the wrong color mode, too—they have no way of dealing with it themselves. Also, as I do not like to send images out without the appropriate calibration, it is a great help to be told what kind of process will be used for final output.

If the final output will be offset litho, we have to look a little closer at things to figure out what the dpi value really needs to be. What kind of paper is being used? If it is an uncoated paper, then the line-screen value of the halftones should probably not be higher than 133 lpi (**NOTE:** that is "lpi"—lines per inch—not "dpi"), otherwise detail will be lost as the dots spread into each other. If, however, you are printing on a coated paper you can usually go straight up to 150 lpi. Some magazine covers go as high as 175 or even 200 lpi, but this is less common. The smaller the dots are, the more fiddly they are to print, and the more often the printer has to stop the presses to clean things up. So, values higher than 150 are only used if they are considered necessary for the quality of the result. In terms of visual effectiveness, most of us pretty much cannot see the dots at 150 lpi, anyway.

The rule of thumb is to double the line-screen value that you are going to end up with and enter that as the dpi at which you want to scan. This is where the magic number of 300 dpi comes from—it is twice the line-screen value of a halftone intended for printing on coated paper. If you have scanned at that value, then obviously you are covered whether you end up printing on coated or uncoated paper, because the actual line-screen of an image is applied by the imagesetter printing the film. So it does not really matter if you have scanned at a slightly higher resolution than you eventually need. All it means is that you merely have a little more detail available within the digital image than you can actually reproduce. It will not be a problem. The problem is when you scan at a resolution that is too low, and therefore pick up less detail than you could potentially print.

The second of the two pieces of information you need, the percentage, can only be determined by you, the designer. Of course, it is quite likely that you will not know at the outset what size you want a particular image to be. This happens to me all the time. I usually make small "for position only" (FPO) scans of everything. They are quick and easy to place, and give me a good enough screen image to work with. When the design is complete, I check to see what the actual scanning percentage needs to be for each image. Here is another tip—I am not at my best when figuring out mathematical problems, so to help I have written the words "divide what you want by what you have" on my calculator. Then I am never too far away from how to figure out a percentage. For example, let us say the original image is 5 $^3/_4$ in (147 mm) wide but the design calls for it to be reduced to 3 $^7/_8$ in (99 mm). If we divide what we want (99) by what we have (147) the answer is 0.6734693. As we do not actually need to scan to seven decimal places, the answer to the question is actually 68%—because it is always best to round the number up, or you may end up with something fractionally smaller than you need.

If I am planning on printing on a mid-range uncoated paper, I could therefore scan it at 266 dpi (2 x 133 lpi) at 68%, and that would give me the optimum scan for the materials being used—no less and no more information than can be reflected in the resulting halftone. If I was planning on printing on coated paper, then it should be scanned at the same percentage but at 300 dpi (2 x 150 lpi).

To sum up: figure out the percentage of enlargement or reduction, then double the desired halftone line-screen value to get the dpi setting. Use that percentage and that dpi value as the scan settings for your image.

Incidentally, while scanners of amazing quality are now available at even more amazing prices, it is worth checking up on the accompanying software before buying, especially the kind of interface that is available if you want to scan directly into Photoshop. Some scanning software aims at the casual user rather than the professional and will give you only a few presets rather than the range of settings you need. If you cannot enter specific dpi and percentage scanning values, you would be better off with a different scanner, however tempting the deal appears to be.

Scanning previously printed images

Occasionally—and hopefully very rarely—you will be sent a print of an image that has been produced using the CMYK process and which you are then supposed to scan and use again for something else.

This scenario presents you with two problems.

The first is one of copyright. Does the client have the right to use this image? If not, and you go ahead and scan it, you may be liable for copyright infringement, too. So definitely check up.

The second problem is that all the correct screen angles for the CMYK colors have already been taken (see chapter 4). If you simply scan the print again, the result will be a moiré pattern. This is because as your scanner moves across the image, it captures whole rows of pixels at a time. Each one of these rows is called a "sample." The number of samples per inch (SPI) is therefore the same as the number of dots, or pixels, per inch that you have specified for the scan. As the scanning "eyes" move across the image, they effectively add a new screen angle made up of the grid formed by all the samples put together. Hence the moiré.

In order to deal with this problem successfully, you have to start with the actual scanning process itself.

If you have a reasonably good scanner, somewhere on it will be settings for a "de-screening" mode. If not, you might as well skip the rest of this chapter because there is nothing that you can do. You can try getting rid of the moiré by applying filters like gaussian blur, median, whatever—and all you will get is a blurred version of the original that has still got a moiré pattern. However, if you have de-screening settings, you have a good chance of ending up with a convincing image. They are usually presented in terms of a list reading something like "art magazine, newsletter, newsprint, custom," and so forth.

What these presets refer to is the density of the line screen in the original image. Selecting one of these determines how much work your scanner will need to do in order to overcome the possibility of a moiré.

It is important to remember that the density of the line screen used in the original print has nothing whatsoever to do with the resolution at which you wish to scan it. Scanning resolution is a completely separate issue that determines how many pixels you want the result to contain. Do not get confused by thinking that if you de-screen at a particular value, then that value is the resolution of your result. All it refers to is the value of the line screen in the original print that your scanner is trying to compensate for when getting rid of the moiré pattern.

If you know the lpi value that was used to print your original, you will hopefully be able to select "custom" from the preset list and enter that number. If you do not know the lpi, you can instead select the item from the list that seems closest to the kind of image you want to scan.

As I mentioned earlier in this chapter, there are standards for line screen values which are used worldwide. For uncoated paper it is 133 or 150 lpi, and for coated stock it is 150, 175, or 200.

However, there is a down-side to this process. Let us say you want to scan an image that is roughly letter-sized, and that is also the size at which you want to end up printing it. Scan settings therefore need to be 300 dpi at 100%. But, since it has also been previously printed on a high-quality coated stock using offset litho, it is safe to assume it is going to have an existing line screen of about 150, possibly more.

If you choose to de-screen at 150 lpi and to simultaneously scan at 300 dpi on an image that is so large to begin with, you could probably go on holiday for a week while the scanner tries to do the work. Most likely your computer will crash because the poor thing will have become completely overloaded.

If this should happen, try the following method, which works on some of the leading brands of scanner. Disregard the lpi value of your original, and instead click on "custom" in the list of de-screening presets. Enter an lpi value of 90, then scan at whatever dpi you want. The results I have produced this way have actually been better than many I have produced using a custom de-screening value of 150 lpi—which often leaves a slight moiré behind. A de-screening value of 90 lpi does not produce a moiré, and best of all, it is quick. To prove it, here is an image prior to de-screening, and then de-screened at both 90 and 150 lpi (fig. **13.1**).

13.1
Left: not de-screened at all.
Center: de-screened at 90 lpi.
Right: de-screened at 150 lpi.

Things get even more interesting if you have a look at the individual channels on a de-screened scan, before and after converting it to CMYK.

RED **GREEN** **BLUE**

13.2
Top row: the RGB channels.
The moiré pattern appears in
the blue channel.
Bottom row: the CMYK
channels. The moiré pattern
appears in the yellow channel.

CYAN **MAGENTA** **YELLOW** **BLACK**

While there was no obvious moiré pattern visible on the de-screened image, something strange is happening within the individual channels while it is still in RGB mode (fig. **13.2**). (Incidentally, to see the information in a single channel, simply click on its name on the drop-down list in the "channels" window.) The red looks OK, so does the green, but in the blue channel, there is a distinct moiré. Now look at the second set of individual channels, which is how things look when the image is converted into CMYK. As you can see, there is a slight moiré in the yellow—which, as previously discussed, does not matter because we cannot see the shape of the yellow dots.

Therefore, the moiré in the blue channel of the RGB image has become the moiré in the yellow channel of the CMYK image—which means that somehow the blue moiré is just as invisible in the RGB image as the yellow moiré is in the CMYK version. Yet blue is visible and the moiré appears to be quite dark and strong—so why can it not be seen?

The answer lies in the way the channels display information in RGB and CMYK.

RGB is showing you light, whereas CMYK is trying to show you pigment. When there is a dark area in, for example, the magenta channel in a CMYK image, it means that magenta is very strong in that part of the image—because in this color mode the channel is showing you how densely the ink will be applied. However, when an area looks quite dark in, for example, the blue channel of an RGB image, it means that there is not much of it present. The lights have been turned down, or off, and so the color will not show as much as it will in a light area.

Therefore it does not matter that there is a moiré which appears as darker dots in the blue channel, because in the visible image that translates to a very slight decrease in the yellow in those areas—and we do not see it.

This is another example of how RGB behaves in the opposite way to the CMY in CMYK. If we want to add yellow to a CMYK image, we increase the strength of the yellow channel. Conversely, if we want to add more yellow to an RGB image we can do it more effectively by reducing the blue—in other words by making the information in the blue channel appear darker. If we try to add yellow by adjusting the red and green channels (i.e. making them appear lighter), we are more likely to create a washed-out result because we will be reducing the red and green components at the same time. However, by adding yellow through an adjustment to the blue channel we can leave the red and green levels—and therefore two-thirds of the colors in the image—unchanged.

Understanding this can be of great help in adjusting a color cast.

The image in fig. **13.3** was sent to me by a client. It was an RGB scan that had somehow been changed, and it was clearly in serious trouble. The client had no idea how it had happened, or how to fix it. All he knew was that he needed it later that same day as part of his presentation for a potentially lucrative property development project.

The first thing to do when you are dealing with a damaged image is to try to identify the biggest problem. After all, if you cannot fix the big problem, it does not matter how many smaller problems you can fix—you still will not have a useable image.

13.3
A rather green cottage.

Looking at this image it was obvious that it was too green. Even so, I have since used this image in lectures and am constantly amazed to hear some of the responses I get to the "what is wrong with this image" question. Too washed-out, over-exposed, not enough red...and while these may be true, if the green-ness cannot be fixed, then any other issues are beside the point.

In fact, pinpointing the problem as a green adjustment turned out to be the key to all the other problems as well.

I decided to check by looking at the individual channels while the image was in RGB mode. Red and blue showed a decent spread of tone, but the green channel was clearly too light (fig. **13.4**). And, this of course translates into an image that is both too light and too green, because, as already discussed, a light area in an RGB channel means that there is more of the color there, i.e. the light of that particular color shines brighter at that point, whereas a light area in a CMYK channel indicates that there is less pigment present.

To fix things, I opened up the "levels" window in Photoshop with just the green channel selected and pulled the "black point" slider over towards the right. The result is shown in fig. **13.5**. The entire solution, from opening the damaged image to re-saving it, took about two minutes.

13.4
Above: the RGB channels, showing a very light green channel (center) which resulted in an image that was too light and also too green.

13.5
The final image, after an adjustment of the green channel.

CHAPTER 14

Trapping

What is trapping?

Trapping is one of those things that most designers do not know about and do not really want to think about. In fact, there is really nothing to it and it is important to bear in mind that, aside from general settings, no one else is likely to take care of it for you. While you can rely on your repro house or printer to deal with trapping to an extent, you cannot expect them to scrutinize every element in your page layout and figure out whether you applied trapping to your Adobe Illustrator or CorelDraw drawings, etc., before importing them—and, unfortunately, it is in imported images of this kind that trapping is often forgotten.

When you have adjacent areas of different colors that are going to be printed by different ink units on a press—for example, a cyan area which touches a magenta area—then unless the registration on the press is perfect (which is almost impossible), the results will not be perfect. In fact they can be seriously unpleasant. Trapping is the means by which a small overlap is applied between the colors which then covers up for the very slight amount of misregistration that you are almost sure to encounter when printing. The way it is best applied depends very much on the software you are using.

One of the important things to know about trapping is that if you do not apply it where it is needed in Illustrator, Corel or Photoshop images, the page-layout software cannot apply it to them afterwards. Nor, except for a few very rare exceptions, can the imagesetter running the subsequent film. As technology continues to advance, trapping will become less of an issue. Even now there are a few RIP systems that can apply trapping to PDF documents intelligently, even when the individual elements in the page layout had no trapping applied to them prior to being imported. This is still extremely uncommon, but if you happen to be using one of the handful of printers worldwide who can do this, make sure you turn off all the trapping settings in all the software you use for your page assembly, otherwise their output method will apply it a second time. For most of us, however, this is not an option. Trapping is still something that needs to be taken care of, and we especially need to apply it to each source file using the software in which it was created. Only then will it be able to carry through to the final page layout.

In Photoshop, you cannot add a trap value unless you are working with a CMYK image, which makes a lot of sense as it is only on a printing press that trapping is important. However, as you add your own traps in Illustrator or Corel, you are not constrained by the same laws and can apply them to RGB-colored elements. This is a pity, and these drawing programs could avoid some of the pitfalls for designers by restricting them to a choice of either CMYK or RGB colors as part of each "new document" set-up.

CorelDraw and Adobe Illustrator examples

I have chosen these rather lurid colors as an example (fig. **14.1**) because they just happen to be two components of the CMYK system and are printed by different ink units on the press. If I were actually picking colors for a two-color print job, I would probably select something much more tasteful from the Pantone book.

In fact, I must admit that I have used these two colors for a design job, straight out of the can. A friend in California asked me to come up with some signs for his real estate business. He wanted "For Sale" signs that people would notice and recognize from half a mile away. If the death threats he has been receiving since they started to appear are anything to go by, I succeeded beyond his wildest dreams!

14.1
The result of misregistration between color elements when no trap has been applied.

Modern printing presses are fantastic pieces of engineering and, in the hands of a good operator, it is possible to put a cyan dot right on top of a magenta dot which is right on top of a yellow dot, and so on. But that is on a good day, with a brand-new press. It is much more likely that the cyan will be ever so slightly out of register with the magenta, which in turn will be ever so slightly out of register with the yellow, etc. The problem is that if you use a drawing program to create an image like the one shown in fig. 14.1, then the hole knocked out of the cyan square is exactly the same size and shape as the magenta circle that is doing the knocking. Given even a small amount of misregistration, the magenta element is almost certain to print with a slight overlap onto the cyan along one side, thus leaving a thin, crescent-shaped white space along the other.

The way to avoid this problem is to produce a very slight overlap between the magenta and cyan shapes. The area both colors then share is known as a trap.

It is not always possible to apply a trap in the way you might want. For example, in this case, if you were using Illustrator or CorelDraw, it would be difficult to trap (i.e. expand) the cyan into the magenta. It could be done, but it would involve much more work. It would be easy, on the other hand, to trap the magenta into the cyan, simply by adding an outline and setting it to overprint. The thing to remember with traps is that it is always best to trap the lighter color into the darker, and not the other way around. If the darker color expanded into the lighter to create the trap, the result would compromise the shape of the lighter-colored object. A good way to remember which way to do this is to imagine the effect, both ways, for yellow type on a black background. Then you will remember that the only thing to do is to trap the yellow into the black, because that is the option which leaves the shape of the type unchanged.

If the overlapping area is small enough, you will not see it. The juxtaposition of two bright colors, especially if they are close to being opposites, slightly dazzles the eye. Thus you would not notice even quite a large overlap—much more than you would want to apply as a trap— because the interaction between the colors, together with the after-image they produce on your retina, would cause you to see a slight optical illusion along their common edge which would make it difficult to see—even if no trap was applied. Alternatively, if the colors are not as bright as my example, or as contrasting, you are not going to see the trap between them simply because they are not bright or contrasting. When you look at an image, you are probably not really looking at detail. It is much more likely that at first you are just getting an overall impression. Maybe then you look a bit closer at the individual elements, but you tend not to investigate the edges where different elements touch, so long as the trap is small enough. Why? Because it is convincing. However, that only works if the trap is small enough to do the job it is intended to do, and not if it is so big that you can easily see it. So, obviously, the amount by which two colors are set to overlap is important.

In Illustrator there are two ways to deal with trapping. One is automatic, one is manual. To create a trap manually, add an outline of 0.25 pt to an object and set it to overprint. You can do this by opening the "attributes" palette and checking "overprint stroke" while the object is selected. To automate trapping between selected objects, use the Pathfinder palette. Select "trap" and enter a width. Again, you will usually want 0.25 pt. You can also specify a tint value to reduce the percentage of the lighter color being trapped, which will make it even less visible.

In CorelDraw, you can also create manual traps between objects by adding a thin outline and setting it to overprint. Select the object, add the outline, then right-click on it and choose "overprint outline." While saving or exporting the file, make sure you have trapping set to "preserve the document overprint settings" (you will find this option if you click on the "advanced" button in the "export" window), otherwise the trapping information will get left behind. This will also be the case if you try to export it as a TIFF. To create automatic traps, you will need to export the drawing as an EPS file. During this process you can click on the "advanced" tab and choose "auto-spreading." The "maximum" command lets you specify the width of the resulting trap.

Incidentally, when using Illustrator or CorelDraw it is also useful to apply "overprint fill" to anything black that runs over an object of another color. As black is the only color that can overlay other colors without creating a visible mix, there is no need to knock out the image beneath it. Therefore, simply allowing it to overprint avoids the need for a trap. The page-layout programs generally allow black to overprint as a default.

Photoshop, InDesign, PageMaker, and Quark

In Photoshop, the default setting is a 1-pixel trap, but of course the size of the pixels is up to you. A 1-pixel trap on a 300 dpi image is ideal for most work. Adobe InDesign's default trap setting is 0.25 pt. InDesign also allows trapping for rich blacks, which is a very sophisticated extra (see "Creating and using a rich black," opposite). Adobe PageMaker's default trap setting is 0.1 mm, which is roughly $1/250$ of an inch. That is generous, but not so much as to cause problems. In Quark, however, the default trap amount is 0.144 pt. Now, if a point is $1/72$ of an inch, then 0.144 of a point is roughly $1/500$ of an inch. If you ask your printers if they can hold registration throughout a four-color run to a $1/500$ of an inch (or just over 0.05 of a millimeter), they will probably laugh at you. To change the default trap settings in Quark, choose "edit/preferences/document/trapping." "Absolute" assigns the given trap amount everywhere it is needed, rather than "proportional," which will alter the amount of trapping depending on the lightness of the color. I suggest setting process trapping to "on" and increasing the default amount to .25 pts. That increases the trap to $1/_{288}$ of an inch—the same as InDesign, and roughly the same as a 1-pixel trap on a 300 dpi image.

In fig. **14.2** I have created three images of a background of solid cyan with a magenta circle in the middle. On the left, it has been generated by CorelDraw and exported as an EPS file with a 1 pt trap. The center image shows the same EPS file but with a 0.25 pt trap. On the right, the same image elements were created in Photoshop as a 300 dpi TIFF file with a 1-pixel trap. (Incidentally, the files for these images were only 220 kb for the vector EPS files, but nearly 1.35 megabytes for the TIFF, so that is clearly one area where vector EPS has an advantage. Of course, given current computer storage capacities it is not such a big deal as it used to be.)

14.2

*Left: CorelDraw EPS, 1 pt trap.
Center: CorelDraw EPS,
0.25 pt trap.
Right: Photoshop 300 dpi
image with 1-pixel trap.*

Do not assign trapping to continuous tone photographic images, because they do not need any. Trapping is only intended for juxtapositions between solid areas of color.

To assign a trap in Photoshop, choose "image/trap." Enter a pixel count and click "OK." A 1-pixel trap on a 300 dpi image will not really be noticeable, even when using it between two colors like cyan and magenta, whereas the alternative—a thin white crescent down one side of the magenta circle—would be very noticeable indeed.

Creating and using a rich black

In the page-layout programs, black is usually set to overprint everything. That makes sense, because black is intended to be opaque and is never trying to create a third color when it overlaps another. Pantone colors are also intended to be opaque. However, this is not the case with cyan, magenta, or yellow, which are intended to be transparent and thus create additional color blends between them when one lands on top of another.

Printing other elements within a large, solid-black background is something which can be fraught with problems. For a start, in order to get a nice solid black, the printer cannot stint on the ink flow. Also, as it is most likely printing onto white paper, there has to be enough of it, evenly spread, if it is going to look even and dense and not patchy. However, if there is a little bit too much of it, set-off might easily occur and ruin the job. This is where the ink on one sheet transfers to the as yet unprinted side of the sheet which lands on top of it in the pile after they have both gone through the press. Both these results are definitely things to avoid.

To complicate matters further, if you have an image in the middle of the solid-black area, then you are creating different ink requirements across your page. This might mean visible streaks unless the coverage is heavy enough to blot them out.

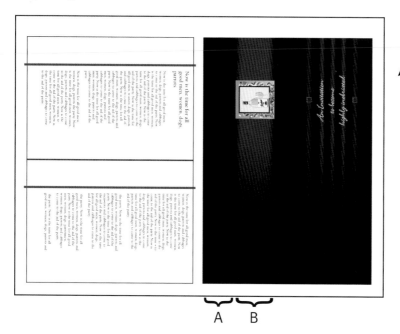

A   B

14.3
There is a different requirement for black ink between sections A and B, which could result in streaking if not enough ink is applied, or set-off if too much is applied.

The example shown in fig. **14.3** shows the sort of thing that might happen. (The arrow indicates the direction of travel through the press.) On either side of the small four-color image on the front cover of the piece (the upper right quarter of the sheet), there is a 100% requirement for black ink, but above and below the area occupied by the image it is closer to 80%. It is therefore quite likely that there will be a visible difference between the black solid in this area and the black solid on either side. The same is true of the lines of type and the small magenta squares, although to a much lesser degree.

The printer is left in a difficult position: either increase the ink flow and risk set-off, or leave the ink flow at a safer, lower level and maybe end up with visible streaks. A good way to avoid this problem is by creating a color called a "four-color black" or "rich black" using whichever of the major drawing, image-adjustment, or page-layout programs you happen to be working in to create the front cover. A "rich black" is a color made up of 100% solid black combined with a supporting tint underneath it. This gives the black the extra density it needs without increasing the flow of ink to a possibly dangerous level. My personal favourite is to put a 45% tint of cyan, plus a 40% magenta and yellow, underneath it. The three colors combine at (almost) equal densities to produce a neutral gray. The result is an even, dense black with no visible pinholes. (There might actually be pinholes, but if there is a 40% tint of gray underneath them, they are almost impossible to spot.) This means less stoppage time on the press, faster turnaround on the job, less quality control further down the production line and, best of all, the potential problems of set-off or a streaky print are avoided. If you create your own rich black, make sure you do not overload the maximum ink density, which has already been discussed in chapter 9.

Some designers prefer to create a more dense black by adding only a 40% cyan, with no yellow or magenta. This makes a good solid black that has a somewhat cool appearance. On the other hand, adding only a 40% magenta—with no cyan or yellow—adds the appearance of red highlights. The effect is quite subtle, but as the addition of another tint enables the printer to lower the density of the black, the color underneath can indeed influence the overall appearance.

Registration and trim marks

The only places where the combined ink density should add up to more than the danger zone—in fact, it should add up to 400%—is in the trim marks and registration targets (fig. **14.4**) that are placed outside the live area of the page and are therefore destined to be cut off and thrown away. The printer can use them to help register the job, and the binding department can use the trim marks to cut and fold it.

These marks are usually added by the imagesetter when it prints out your film. You can add them yourself if you are designing something smaller than a letter-sized page that is going to be printed on its own—a custom shape, for example, or a matrix of business cards—but they will be of no use around the edge of an advertisement that will be dropped onto a larger layout, as any marks you add will just be cut off. You can easily create your own vector registration mark in Illustrator and save it as a small four-color EPS file. Or, you can create the same thing as a 1200 dpi black-and-white bitmap image in Photoshop, which can be colored by specifying it as "registration" (which is made up of all four process colors at 100%) in page-layout programs. For trim marks, just use a hairline drawn in the page layout, again specified in "registration" color. If you want it to indicate a fold, use a dotted hairline, but write "fold" next to it, so it is the printer's fault if they cut along it by mistake!

14.4
A printer's registration "target."

Trapping into a rich black

The greatest difficulty arising from the use of a rich black is in trapping with other elements. For an example, imagine a brochure that has a solid black cover with a line of white type running across it. If a rich black is used, there will be a registration problem around the edge of the white type. It will probably have a thin cyan line visible along one edge, and perhaps magenta visible along another, and a faint hint of yellow on yet another.

Fig. **14.5** shows a scenario that is very common. However, there are ways of getting around this situation.

14.5
Due to misregistration, the other colors present in the rich black can be seen around the edges of the white lettering.

For users of Quark, Illustrator and CorelDraw, the solution is one that printers do not like at all and will try to dissuade you from using. Try not to be put off. I have used the following method more times than I can remember, and it has never yet failed. The idea is to send the printer two copies of the final file. From file one, tell the printer to only run the black film (or plate if using CTP). The second version is an exact copy of the first with one exception: a white outline has been added to the type, thereby forcing all four colors away from it. Tell the printer to run only the cyan, magenta and yellow films (or plates) from this file.

So long as the printer does not run the black film (or plate) on Monday and then wait until the following Friday to run the other three colors—which could mean that the images on the two sets will not match perfectly because of various environmental differences—then the chances of them not fitting are no more than when running all the separations from a single file. However, that is unlikely to prevent your printer from predicting dire consequences. It is quite likely that they will not have been asked to do this before, and one thing printers really dislike is a nasty surprise coming off the end of the press, especially if they might be held liable. Nevertheless, if you manage to persuade them to go ahead, the results will probably be one of the nicest things they ever printed. As a result, your standing with them will probably rise to such a point that you will get the red-carpet treatment from them from then on.

NOTE: You can still use a digital proof when using this method, because you can run it from the first of the two files. Even though it is not exactly the configuration that will actually run on the press, none of the color values will be any different.

The method described above has been used to create fig. **14.6**, which is a CMYK image using a rich black in which the word "Balloonist" has had a white outline added in the magenta, cyan and yellow components.

In Illustrator and CorelDraw, this is quite easy to do. In Quark, it is rather more difficult because you cannot add white outlines to type until it has been converted into a graphic image. To do this, highlight the text with the "content" tool and then choose "style/text to box." Unfortunately, Quark does not convert your existing type into a graphic but creates a duplicate that is placed adjacent to the original. So, you will end up with three copies of the job instead of two. The first will contain the original editable type. In the second copy the type will have been converted into a box (and repositioned), but no outline will have been applied. In the third, which is an exact copy of the second, the white outline has been added. (To do this, use the "colors" window to apply white as the outline color, then specify the outline width using "item/frame.") The second and third copies of the file are then sent to the printer, the second file being used to generate only the black and the third to generate the C, M, and Y.

Because the black is reasonably opaque, no one will ever notice that right around the edge of the type there is an area which is not quite as dense as the rest of the background. For one thing, it is a very thin area. For another, there is a high degree of visible contrast. The eye will be slightly dazzled by the brightness of the type against the dark background, and so it will not see the tiny "trap" area.

For users of PageMaker, this method will not work as it is impossible to add a white outline to type.

For users of InDesign, the news regarding rich black is very good. InDesign contains a trapping engine that allows the user to specify the width of a "hold-back" setting. This keeps the supporting screens of the other colors away from the edges of reversed or light elements, so that they retain their sharpness in the final print. In other words, it traps a rich black perfectly.

CHAPTER 15

Using Pantone Colors

The Pantone Matching System

Most designers who have sent their work to print shops have, at one time or another, run across Pantone Matching System (PMS) colors. These are colors which printers can mix using the formula written under each sample in the swatch book.

While the formula is designed to give the same result every time, there are invariably slight variations between one mix and another. Therefore, if you plan on using the same color repeatedly over time and want a high degree of consistency throughout, you may want to talk to the printer about mixing up a large batch and storing it for you for future use. You will save on mixing charges and consistency will be improved, especially if you request that density readings are taken and matched to approved samples each time the color is run.

The PMS range can be mixed from a range of several "standard" colors which come straight out of a can. These include not only the four process colors but also colors like Pantone Green, Pantone Purple, Pantone Orange, Rubine Red, Reflex Blue, and others. Therefore, the range of colors it is possible to mix goes way beyond a range limited to combinations of just C, M, Y, and K.

Thus, when you are trying to match a PMS color using CMYK inks, you are very likely to run into just the same problem as when starting with an RGB color: you cannot do it.

PMS colors are, however, ideal for two-color work and duotones. As I mentioned before, if you do not have a swatch book yourself—and they are quite expensive—your local print shop probably will. As well as making them available for client use, they probably upgrade them from time to time, and if so they might be persuaded to sell (or give) you the old ones. Despite dire warnings from the manufacturers, it takes several years for the colors to fade even slightly, especially if you keep them in a dark drawer somewhere. Just to be sure, check any older books you are planning on using against a new one.

Most of the difficulties I have run into concerning the use of Pantone Matching System colors fall within one of the following three scenarios.

choose "select/modify/contract" and enter a value of 1 pixel. Then select the other channels one by one and delete the information within the selected area. This ensures a small trap between the CMYK and the Pantone colors.

If the Pantone color is a tint, not a solid, then further complications arise. This is because there are no more available screen angles for another color. As we have seen (see chapter 4), there are not actually enough screen angles for the CMYK colors, and they only work together without producing a visible moiré pattern because of the unusual visual properties of yellow (you can see its color, but you cannot see its shape).

The solution here is again to generate a selection based on the spot channel (and again reduce that selection by 1 pixel to create a trap) and then knock it out of either the cyan, magenta or black channels. Then you can assign the same screen angle to the Pantone tint as was occupied by the color you have knocked out. The reason you cannot do this in the yellow channel is, of course, because printing your Pantone color at the yellow screen angle will produce a visible moiré. Only colors like process yellow are able to produce moiré patterns that we cannot actually see.

Regardless of whether the Pantone color is a solid or a tint, you will need to save the result as a DCS2 (desktop color separation 2) image. As it is an EPS format, you will be prompted to choose the image header type. For the best screen image, choose an 8-bits-per-pixel TIFF preview (which will translate into 256 colors on screen) and a "DCS with Color Composite (72 pixels/inch)." PC users should save with the ASCII option, Mac users with Binary.

Then, when you import the result into Quark, InDesign, or PageMaker, you will see a color image which incorporates your Pantone channel, and the Pantone color will be able to generate a separate piece of film in addition to the CMYK separation.

NOTE: Do not forget to tell the printer/repro house the screen angle which should be applied to the Pantone color.

NOTE: If you are sending files to your printer in PDF format, even for CTP printing, DCS2 images can be included. If, for example, a one-page layout containing a DCS2 file (which includes a Pantone spot channel) is converted to PDF using Distiller (rather than the "file/export" option found in PageMaker or InDesign) and "separations" are picked as an option in the "color" section of the print dialogue window, the Pantone can be told to print as well as the CMYK colors. When the result is viewed in Acrobat Reader there will be five pages, one for each of the CMYK components and one for the Pantone. As each of these can be used to generate a plate, they can be used in a CTP operation provided it is a five-color run. If only a four-color run is wanted, one of the "separations" options is to convert spot colors to process.

Incidentally, when asking a printer for a price on a job that uses one of the Pantone standard colors (the ones that come straight out of the can), remember to mention that there should not be any mixing charge added for the Pantone color. It always helps to let printers know that you know what you are talking about.

Other Pantone products

While the Pantone Matching System guide is probably the most commonly encountered member of the Pantone range, there are several other swatch books that will be of enormous help to graphic designers. To see them all, visit www.pantone.com.

The metallic formula guide

This is similar to the PMS swatch book but much smaller, with only 204 colors. The metallic range provides a beautiful and exotic set of mixes between straight-out-of-the-can metallic inks and PMS colors, and the results on press can be amazing. However, the ability of metallic inks to be reflective—and there is not much point in using a metallic ink if it is not allowed to be reflective—relies on a hard, smooth, coated paper surface. You cannot expect to get the same results from an uncoated stock, especially if it also has a textured finish. Some kinds of varnish can have a detrimental effect on the metallic appearance, but fortunately the swatch book offers both varnished and unvarnished samples of each color. However, it is also possible to use a varnish to increase the effectiveness of a metallic ink by first printing it on those areas which will then be overprinted with the metallic. To be most effective, the varnish should be a "spot" rather than a "flood" application, so that it only underprints the metallic area and not the entire sheet. The varnish will then help to seal the sheet, allowing the metallic to be more reflective, while not changing the appearance of the paper surface elsewhere.

Pantone metallic shades are much closer to being completely opaque than Pantone Matching System colors, simply because of the opacity of the metallic element.

Obviously there are many other intermediate mixes which can be extrapolated from the formulas given in the swatch book. If your clients want a shade that is not represented, it should not be too hard to come up with a mix that lands between the two swatches closest to the desired color. Just make sure they agree beforehand that the responsibility for heading into such uncharted territory is theirs, and not yours!

The pastel formula guide
With 126 colors, this is even smaller than the metallic guide. Each pastel color swatch in the book comes complete with two tear-out chips. Pantone has developed a base palette specifically for this pastel range in order to make it easier for printers to mix consistently accurate pastel colors with a minimum of waste.

CHAPTER 16

Photoshop Tips and More

Changing an object's color

I almost did not write this chapter as there are already so many excellent books around which can show you how to do incredible things with Photoshop. However, there are a few methods that I have found to be extremely useful but have not yet seen mentioned in any of the books I have read, so I thought it would be worthwhile to include them here.

Most Photoshop users will have already experimented with adjusting the color of an object using one method or another, but in general these are somewhat hit-and-miss. There is, however, a less well-known method which will allow you to accurately change the color of an object while preserving all the highlight and shadow information at the same time.

Let us take an example of a fairly typical, red London double-decker bus (fig. **16.1**).

16.1
The original image.

How about if you wanted to make it green—but not just any green, something very specific: C: 85%, M: 15%, Y: 95%, K: 10%?

First, set those percentages as the foreground color. Then open the "layers" window and create a new transparent layer. Fill it with your new foreground color, and then select "hue" as the blending mode (fig. **16.2**) from the drop-down list in the layers window.

16.2
The original image, plus a second layer filled with the specified color and set to a blending mode of "hue."

The bus turns green. So, unfortunately, does everything else which had a discernable hue—but notice that if something was a neutral color beforehand, it still is. You can also make this kind of change using "color" as the blending mode, which colors everything in the image, whereas "hue" only colors things that were non-neutral. "Color" mode also tends to give less contrast between shadows and highlights.

You will then need to use the "eraser" tool, or a selection, or a mask to delete the new color from the areas in which it is not needed. If you erase the green color from an area where you wanted to keep it, simply paint it back in using the paintbrush tool with an opacity of 100%. When you are happy with the result, flatten the layers and save (fig. **16.3**).

16.3
The final image, a very convincing green bus.

The advantage of using this method over other coloring options is that you can specify an exact tint which becomes the basis for the entire tonal range within an object, thus creating a very convincing result.

Smooth gradients

The "gradient" tool in Photoshop is one of my all-time favorite painting tools. Prior to digital methods, creating a gradient required all kinds of messing around in a darkroom. First, you needed either an airbrushed piece of artwork—and it was not easy (or cheap) to get one painted with a really smooth gradient—or you had to create one photographically by using lights and an angled backdrop, usually a huge roll of paper several yards wide. Either way, the result had to replace the existing background in the photo in question, which meant painting a mask (with no possibility of anti-aliasing) and making double exposures onto yet another piece of film. At every stage of the process great care had to be taken to ensure that the highlights did not burn out, nor the shadows burn in. It was all very complicated. This was territory only ventured into by the qualified or the foolish, and only the qualified emerged with a usable result.

In Photoshop it is all so much easier. Isolate your object by selecting and deleting unwanted areas, then decide on your foreground and background colors. Create a new layer, place it behind the original and click and drag the cursor across it to determine the start and end points for your gradient.

But there are still a couple of things it is useful to know.

Unless you take care to avoid it, you can end up with visible "banding" across the tinted area. This is typically caused by, for example, filling an area with a very subtle tint that only contains a small number of shades of a color. Oddly enough, the way to avoid it is by adding "noise" to the layer containing the gradient (fig. **16.4**). The noise filter acts a bit like an editable dither. It scatters the pixels around, and can easily create a "sandblasted" effect if over-applied because it also changes the hue and contrast levels of individual pixels. At full strength it produces a chaotic mass of primary and secondary colors. However, if it is used to dither the pixels very slightly, it simply removes visible banding and makes a gradient even smoother. I usually apply a setting of 3 if I am working with a 300 dpi image. If you zoom in after applying it, close enough to see the individual pixels, you will see that your gradient has been jiggled around just a bit. Despite the apparently rougher appearance, it will now print smoother than before.

16.4
On the left, a standard blend. On the right, the same blend but with a noise value of 3 applied.

The other important thing to know is that, whenever possible, it is best to add gradients to images *after* changing the color mode to CMYK. If you add them in RGB mode and then convert the image, they will not be quite as smooth.

One day you will probably find yourself faced with having to use an image that has not only been provided by the client in RGB mode but is filled with what are obviously bright RGB colors.

If you try changing the mode to CMYK, all these RGB colors will immediately become their closest CMYK equivalent, which might, of course, not look anything like the original. That is because in order to find the appropriate CMYK color, Photoshop simply reverses the polarity of the percentages of RGB and renders those values as the new CMY(K) shade. So, if the RGB color was made up of red and green completely off and blue completely on, it becomes instead a CMY color made up of C and M (almost) completely on and Y completely off. The result is that on screen the color turns from being an intense, glowing blue to being a dark, bluish-purple. Nevertheless, as far as Photoshop is concerned, it has done a good job with the conversion.

If your image contains a mix of colors that are both inside and outside the CMYK range, and only those colors outside it change when you convert the image, it can obviously lead to a very unbalanced result.

To avoid this, do not make the color-mode conversion immediately. While the image is still in RGB mode, choose "image/adjustments/hue & saturation," and then gently reduce the saturation level. As you do so, you are pulling all the RGB colors in the image back towards the CMYK

Using desaturation to avoid RGB problems

range. The image is adjusted holistically because you are working on everything at once, and this means your image maintains the overall balance it had to begin with. Best of all, you get to decide where you want the process to stop, which is how you should approach all your image adjustments.

NOTE: If you only want to desaturate certain ranges of color in your image, try selecting them by using "select/color range." It is an excellent method that can give much better and more convincing results than by using the magic wand tool.

Useful grayscale options

If you ever need to generate a grayscale image from an RGB original, you might want to consider whether you want the morning, noon or evening version (fig. **16.5**).

This will not work with a CMYK image because the color information is spread between the channels in a completely different way, but if you are starting with an RGB version of a picture taken outdoors, and especially if there is a blue sky in the image, it might work very well.

In the mornings, blue light tends to be strongest and most visible. That is why morning light tends to look cooler. Towards the middle of the day neither blue- nor red-light densities have the upper hand, so things even out. Then, as the sun goes down, red light becomes stronger. You can use this to your advantage by simply opening up the "channels" window and clicking on the channels, one by one. As you do so, the image will appear as the grayscale image contained in that channel.

(If the channels do not appear in grayscale but in color, go to "edit/ preferences/display & cursors" and de-select "channels in color" in the top left corner.)

When you have made your choice, simply convert the image into grayscale format, calibrate it according to the printing method you need to use, and save.

NOTE: Because the calibration method described in chapter 7 retains all the tone information in the image, it is possible to adjust the settings more than once. For example, if an image is needed for printing on coated stock, it could first be calibrated for that and subsequently re-calibrated for an uncoated-paper press run at a later date.

16.5

Top: The "morning" version, i.e. the blue channel.

Center: The "midday" version, i.e. the green channel.

Bottom: The "evening" version, i.e. the red channel.

"Unsharp mask" and LAB mode

Most users of Photoshop will have made use of the "sharpening" filters from time to time. I have often met designers who prefer the presets of "sharpen" and "sharpen more" because they seem to do a reasonable job, whereas they have noticed that the use of "unsharp mask" tends to cause light or dark edges around things. Unfortunately, because our screens are more forgiving than the average printing press, if you see this effect even slightly on screen you can guarantee that it will appear to be much more pronounced in print. However, if it is used in the right way, unsharp mask is actually by far the best sharpening filter available.

The reason why these edges appear is due to the way in which a sharpening filter works. Not surprisingly, Photoshop cannot actually sharpen an image so that you will see more detail than existed before. Instead, it searches for edges within the image and boosts the contrast level alongside them. The effect is as if we can suddenly see the detail more clearly. It is yet another illusion, but it can be very convincing.

Unsharp mask is the only sharpening filter that I use, because it is editable. It therefore puts me in control of the level of adjustment that I want to make. Given that the printing press is going to accentuate whatever I do with the filter, I always take care not to sharpen to the point of clearly seeing those high-contrast edges. This is basically a matter of experience, and the only thing to do if you do not have very much is to go carefully. However, there are a couple of other things that can help.

Unsharp mask uses three different settings: "threshold," "radius," and "amount." The threshold determines which colors within the image will be affected by the adjustment. A setting of o levels means that everything will be sharpened. The radius slider determines how far away from the edges the sharpening effect will spread. If you hold this to between 1 and 1.5 pixels, those high-contrast halos will be much smaller and therefore harder to see. Lastly, the amount is the strength of the sharpening itself. Holding the radius to a lower level enables a higher level of sharpening to be applied without running into problems.

Using these settings will immediately improve your results, but here is another very good method that can be used at the same time.

If you are applying the sharpening to the whole image, then all the colors in all the channels are being worked on simultaneously. However, the sharpness of an image relies much more on the relative lightness and darkness of tone than it does on the color information. If the colors can be left out while the sharpening is done, they will not be included in any resulting distortion around edges within the image. This, too, will cut down on visible halos.

In order to do this, the image must first be converted into **LAB** mode.

LAB is actually the widest color space available, even slightly bigger than RGB. Therefore you can convert into LAB mode and back again without changing any color data in your image, no matter where you start from. In other words, it is a safe mode. The name "LAB" comes from the names given to the three color channels that make up a LAB image: "lightness," "A," and "B." The lightness channel holds all the detail in the image in terms of light and shade. Channels A and B hold all the color information. If you mess around with the A and B channels, you will park your image up a tree faster than you can believe, but for those who want to know, the A channel holds all the color information for areas that contain red or green. Green shows up as darker-than-50% gray, red as lighter. Non-red and non-green areas show up as a neutral 50% gray. The B channel does the same thing for blue and yellow (fig. **16.6**).

16.6
The channel components of an image in LAB mode: "lightness" (left) and "A" and "B" (below).

By clicking on the lightness channel in the channels window, and then applying unsharp mask, you can apply sharpening to a much greater degree than would otherwise be possible. Then simply convert the image back into either RGB or CMYK (fig. **16.7**).

16.7
The original image in CMYK mode.

To show the kind of distortion that sharpening in CMYK mode can lead to, here are two examples (fig. **16.8**). Both have been oversharpened in order to make the differences between them easier to see. In the top image, all four CMYK channels were sharpened simultaneously using a radius setting of 10 and an amount setting of 200. In the bottom image, the same settings were used, but they were only applied to the lightness channel while the image was in LAB mode. The contrast is the same in both images, but the additional color distortion can clearly be seen in the top image.

16.8
The image sharpened in CMYK mode with the "radius" setting at 10 and the "amount" at 200.

The image sharpened with a "radius" setting of 10 and an "amount" of 200, but only in the "lightness" channel in LAB mode. This results in a similar increase in contrast but no distortion of color values.

Fig. **16.9** shows a much healthier image. Once again sharpening was only applied to the lightness channel in LAB mode, but this time with a radius setting of 1 and an amount of 200.

16.9
A "radius" setting of 1 and an "amount" of 200 applied to the "lightness" channel in LAB mode.

NOTE: If your image was RGB to begin with, and you convert it first to LAB mode and from there into CMYK, it is just the same as if you had gone from RGB directly to CMYK: you will effectively be forcing an uncontrolled conversion from the one to the other. As I have said, this is something to be avoided until you know you will be happy with the result.

Choosing the right halftone dot shape

As you can see in fig. 16.9, the quality of the result when using unsharp mask depends very much on a low radius setting and whether the color within the image is included in the adjustment or left out.

Round dots are fine for almost every application, but there might be occasions when an oval, or perhaps a diamond dot, will produce a better print. The reason for this is because of what happens when two dots meet.

As dot size increases, the point at which they touch gets closer and closer. As this happens, the percentage of the tint increases. When they actually touch, they grab onto each other as if they were long-parted friends. This creates a **tint jump**, and several percentage points of tint value are lost as a result (fig. **16.10**).

If you happen to be printing an image in which the middle-range color values are particularly important—Caucasian flesh tones, for example—and you want to get as much out of the tint range as you possibly can, an oval dot would be a better choice than a round dot.

This is because the single tint jump that happens when using a round dot is divided into two smaller tint jumps when you use an oval dot.

Round dots suddenly join up on four sides, but oval dots first collide at each end, and then further towards the shadows, they overlap at the top and bottom as well (fig. **16.11**).

16.10

The "tint jump" when using a round dot.

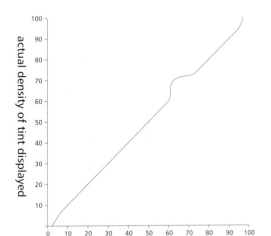

16.11

For an oval dot, the "tint jump" is divided into two smaller ranges.

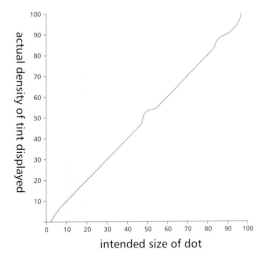

The result is a small tint jump slightly to the highlight side of the midtones, and another small tint jump out towards the shadows. The area between these is where most of the flesh tones will print.

Diamond dots are actually square, but if we were using just one color—black—we would set the screen at an angle of 45°, therefore all the squares would be tipped onto one corner (fig. **16.12**)—hence "diamond."

This shape allows completely even tone reproduction right up to around 90% density, then suddenly everything fills in completely. The dots join up not at single points but along whole sides. So, it is a very good shape to use for images that do not have any dense shadow areas.

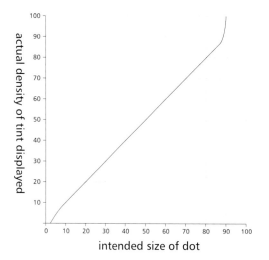

16.12
A diamond dot does not create a "tint jump" until the darker shadow areas are reached, but then it fills in completely.

NOTE: Usually the dot shape is a feature of imagesetter printing rather than something to deal with yourself, so it is important to tell the printer where you want it applied.

CHAPTER 17

Preparing the File for the Printer

A printing checklist

When the final design has been approved by the client and all the production work has been completed, it is time to send the job out to the printer.

This is when you will be really happy if you have done everything possible to prepare things for the press, because then you will not spend the next few nights waking up at 3 A.M. worrying about the job.

Obviously, most of the book so far has been intended to help you prepare things correctly. Even so, despite taking great care every step of the way, it is still alarmingly easy for mistakes to get through. From personal experience I can honestly say that hitting "file/save" for the last time is not the time to relax. It is time for a clear head—and a detailed checklist.

The last thing you want is for an error to get through which means that everyone can point to you. So, as well as checking your own work as far as is possible, it is also important to communicate very clearly with your printer so that there are no gray areas of responsibility that could come back to haunt you. This in turn means that anything you set up with the printer verbally should be backed up in writing. Remember, too, that a little more information than was needed is infinitely preferable to a little less than was needed.

Image checklist

All images must be CMYK-TIFF or CMYK-EPS (i.e. EPS, DCS2 or PDF) format. No RGB, and no GIFs, JPEGs, BMPs (windows bitmaps) or PSDs.

No redundant alpha channels. These are additional channels that are sometimes added to images in order to save selections or create masks. If you leave them in place, they will confuse many imagesetters and generally screw things up. They are extremely useful tools for image creation, but just remember to remove them.

No clipping paths, except where they are really needed. If you do need them, check that the pages in your document which contain such images print successfully on a PostScript printer *before* you send the job out.

Bleeds: images that need to run off the page should extend at least $\frac{1}{8}$ in (3 mm) beyond the page boundaries, except on the binding where they should end at the edge of the page.

If the images are linked rather than embedded, make sure that you send the images to the printer as separate files.

If the images are embedded rather than linked, it is still a good idea to send them. If something corrupts an embedded image, having to send out a new copy will hold everything up.

Check that the images which appear in the final file are the correct high-resolution versions, and not low-resolution "for position only" copies.

Make sure that the written information accompanying the job lists all the images, whether linked or embedded, by their actual filenames. If you are working on a PC, this will also indicate the format (.tif, .eps, etc.). If you are working on a Mac, you should also indicate which image files are in what format.

Text checklist

Make sure, beforehand, that the printer has all the fonts needed to print the job.

Check that there are no surprise fonts associated with the page-layout file, because even if they do not actually appear in your work, it might hold things up while everyone tries to figure out what is happening. If there are fonts that you did not intend to use but that occupy blank line spaces, you should go through the job and change their specification to fonts you have actually used. Otherwise the file will put up an error message as it is trying to open, and this is likely to delay things while the printer tries to contact you to sort things out. If there is not time for you to do this, tell the printer to expect Arial (or whatever) to show up as a required font, but that it will not be a problem as it is only applied to blank line spaces. Therefore nothing will get through onto the film except the leading value associated with that line of type, which will remain the same no matter what the typeface defaults to.

Make sure that the required fonts are listed in the information you send with the job. Even though it is unlikely to be very useful, let the printer know the format (i.e. PostScript, TrueType, etc.) of the fonts you have used.

General checklist

In your page-layout file, check that any graphic elements you have created are not outlined or filled with RGB colors. Also, if you added new swatches to the page-layout color styles, make sure that they are specified as "process" rather than "spot" colors, otherwise they will want to output either as a separate sheet of film or an additional plate.

If the job includes a "spot" varnish, i.e. a varnished area that is a distinct shape rather than a "flood" varnish, which goes everywhere, it is a good idea to include the information in the form of an additional Pantone color. Tell the printer, in writing, that the Pantone actually represents the varnish area and is not intended to print in color.

If you have run type across an image or a background color, check that it is easily readable—remembering that it only takes a very tiny degree of frustration to make someone turn the page and go on to something else.

Print out a complete copy of your job and send it with the digital files.

If the job requires folding, also send in an actual size folding dummy: a full-size folded model of the entire job. Best is if it is on the same, or a very similar, paper stock to the one you will actually be using. In your file, cuts should be indicated by solid lines outside the live area, and folds should appear as dotted lines—and it does not hurt to type "cut" or "fold" (outside the live image area, of course) next to the appropriate line.

Folds are sometimes scored beforehand, especially if the stock is quite heavy and/or it is going to be folded against the grain. If you are using a fairly heavy paper but the printers have not spoken to you about scoring the job, it is possible that they have forgotten to factor this into their estimate. In this case you should ask them whether the folds will be against or with the grain on the press and if that might cause problems.

At the print shop
Things to do when getting an estimate for a job
If you have not used a particular print shop before, ask them to send you some representative samples of their work, well before you actually face a heavy deadline. You do not want them to only send the best things they ever did, because they will not be indicative of the quality level you can fairly expect. You need to see samples of the kind of quality they produce every day.

Proofs
Decide what kind of proof you need. Remember, the better the proof (i.e. the closer it looks to what will eventually come rolling off the end of the press), the more it will cost. Most printers will only offer one or two of the following alternatives:

1) Best—and therefore most expensive—are wet proofs, run from the actual plates which will be used to print the job. These will give you the closest approximation to how the job should eventually look.

2) Next best—and therefore next most expensive—are laminate proofs like Cromalins and **Matchprints**. These are made up of four extremely thin sheets of film, each of which holds one of the color components of the CMYK separation (in the appropriate color), all laminated to a bright white backing sheet. The image on each sheet is created using toner rather than ink.

As this kind of proof is produced from the film that has been generated from a digital or mechanical file, they can show trapping, mis-registration, color casts—almost everything that is wrong with the job—except for the dot gain that will take place when the ink hits the paper. They quite often show tiny "blips" of pure CMYK color here and there, and it is always a good idea to bring them to the printers' attention as being possible errors on the film. They are probably not, but it is always better to check.

Obviously, if you are using CTP for your printing output, generating either a Cromalin or Matchprint proof will require outputting the film that a CTP workflow is intended to avoid. For this reason, both these methods are losing more and more of the proofing market worldwide to digital proofing as time goes by. Nevertheless, they produce very accurate proofs and are sometimes available in a wide range of Pantone Matching System colors as well as the usual CMYK.

3) Digital proofs are a much cheaper mid-range proof and are gaining in popularity worldwide. Even though they cannot show, for example, how effective your trapping has been, the cost factor alone has meant that they are edging other more expensive methods out of the market.

4) Inkjet proofs can be very accurate, especially if they have been run on a machine with a PostScripting function, otherwise all the EPS files will print as "image header" low-resolution TIFFs. Also, colors tend to be rather bright and saturated on some inkjets, especially if they are using pigmented inks. These are a very exciting development for the digital artist, as the colors are extremely resistant to fading, but as they also have a wider gamut than conventional CMYK inks, things tend to look "pumped up"—and again, trapping ceases to be apparent due to their perfect color registration. Best among the inkjet proofs are **Iris** prints which are generated on a PostScript inkjet printer and produce colors close enough to SWOP standards for many to accept them as contract proofs.

Work that has been proofed using Cromalins, Matchprints, and inkjet machines tends to look a bit brighter than it will on the actual press run because all three methods use a very bright white background, much whiter than most paper stocks can ever hope to be—and that is definitely something you should warn your client about beforehand.

5) The worst kind of proofs are pages that have been run from a color laser printer. These, while being the cheapest proofing option, can be so bad in terms of color accuracy that they are misleading. In this case they are worse than useless and should only be looked at for basic positioning and typographical errors.

Things to back up in writing
I always request that the printer (or repro house) should call immediately if there are any problems. *Immediately*. If you do not get feedback in a timely fashion, you may miss deadlines. Because this is so important to me, I tell printers that if they fail to contact me as soon as they run into a problem, then unfortunately I will not be able to work with them again.

Make sure that the written information tells the printer the size of the job in terms of page dimensions and numbers, and how many ink colors are required. If you are using Pantone colors, list them by name. Ideally when ordering anything other than black-and-white work, you should send in a color print of your file rather than a single-color laser proof.

Check with your printer about trapping. This is particularly important if you are creating a high-resolution PDF file which may be impossible to edit later on.

Quantity, paper stock, price, and terms of delivery should be detailed on the written quote the printer has supplied to you. However, it is very common for a range of quantities and prices to have been given. Confirm in writing which options you have decided on *before* work begins.

Ask the printer to make sure type has not reflowed before going to the trouble of running a proof. This is especially important if the proof relies on generating film. I once sent out the file for a 700-page book and forgot to mention this. The type reflowed—only a very small amount, it is true— but by the time it came to the end of chapter three, the last line could not fit on the page and instead jumped to the first page of chapter four. The rest of the film for the book was therefore scrap, at $8 a page.

Is the job date-specific? If so, make sure the printers know that they cannot be late.

Confirm the number of copies you need to receive.

Confirm that the film is to be specified on the invoice if it is likely to be important to you later on.

(For more information on these last two points, see "Tools of the Trade" later in this chapter.)

U sing Adobe Acrobat is another area where graphic designers tend to sit back in the hope that someone else will take care of it. However, printers all over the world are starting to tell their clients that they can no longer accept Quark, PageMaker, or InDesign files and that instead high-resolution PDF format files are the only thing they will be able to work with in the future.

Using Adobe Acrobat

There are good economic reasons for this. In order to deal with "native" file formats, printers and repro houses have to maintain a substantial knowledge base among their employees in order to deal with a very wide range of work. They need to know how to use all the software the designer has used, and they have to know how to spot problems and fix them.

Consider the amount of work you have to do in order to get a PageMaker, QuarkXpress, or InDesign (or whatever) file completely ready to send to a print shop. Anything that has not been done correctly can create problems for the printer, and this is why printers prefer work that comes to them completely finished and ready to roll.

The downside, from the designer's point of view, is that PDF files are generally un-editable. Certain things can sometimes be changed, especially with Acrobat 6, which allows more post-creation editing than previous versions. Otherwise, you might be able to move some elements a little, and sometimes edit type to a degree, but in most cases you are out of luck. Trapping on imported images, calibrating images, problems with color—all these generally need be taken care of beforehand.

Fortunately, Acrobat is not a difficult program. Basically, it is a virtual printer that has a few other settings, too. The main thing is to be somewhat methodical and to work through the process carefully, keeping the desired end result in mind.

When using Acrobat, you can create anything from a low-resolution RGB file suitable for on-screen viewing (these can also include hyperlink information and are often used to produce things like digital software manuals with an interactive table of contents) to a high-resolution file complete with crisp CMYK images that is completely ready for the printer. You can include bleeds, crop marks, printer's marks, everything you need —including fonts, embedded in the file, and even Pantone colors.

There are two basic options available when creating a PDF: Acrobat Distiller and Acrobat PDF Writer. Both allow you to produce an accurate image of your finished art in a format that can be readily understood by both PCs and Macs. More importantly, it is a format that can be printed by imagesetters. PDF Writer turns a file into a PDF; Distiller turns a PostScript file into a PDF. Which one you use depends partly on your own preference and partly on the success of the installation. Distiller will invariably show up in the "installed printers" list, whereas PDF Writer might not, despite being repeatedly installed until everyone concerned is blue in the face. It does not matter. Distiller does a great job and sometimes gives you options not found in PDF Writer.

NOTE: If you are trying to create a PDF from a file that contains spot colors in the form of DCS2 files, read the end of "Typical scenario 3" in chapter 15. Normal CMYK and grayscale EPS files however should not need any special treatment.

It is possible that an EPS image will prevent the successful creation of a PDF file on your system. If that happens, you will need to either re-create it, perhaps as a TIFF file, or leave it out. If it will not print on your PostScript printer (in this case, Acrobat), then it will not print on your printer's imagesetter, either.

If you are using either PageMaker or InDesign, you are in luck. As Acrobat is also an Adobe product, it can interface with both these programs in a slightly smoother way than just about everything else. Any program from which you can print will show Distiller and/or PDF writer as printer options, but PageMaker and InDesign allow you to choose "file/export/Adobe PDF" instead.

I am not going to go into all the possibilities here; there are plenty of books available that will take you through every option. I am just going to concentrate on the ones that are particularly important for graphic designers who want to output high-res files for their print shop.

You will need to have a PostScript printer already installed on your system—Mac or PC—before you can use Acrobat to create a PDF file.

PageMaker

Using the "export" option opens the "PDF options" window. This allows you to choose one of the preset distiller settings, determine the page size for the job and the printer style.

If you edit the distiller preset that you select, you will need to save the new settings under a custom name. Then, of course, you will have it ready to use again in the future. To edit the settings, click on the "edit job options" button in the "distiller settings" part of the window.

Here is how to decide which preset to use. If you are sending someone the resulting PDF document as an e-mail attachment, the preset you probably want is "screen." If you are sending the file to a digital printer, choose "eBook," which allows for 150 dpi images. If you are sending the file to a printer either for CTP or offset printing, choose "print." All of these will probably need editing slightly to do exactly what you want.

The page size options (under the "pages" section) can either be that of the current document or based on the current printer style. This is very important if you have any bleeds in the job. If you do not, then obviously the current document page size is fine. If you do, It must be changed or it will cut them all off. To allow for a bleed, cancel out of the current operation and go to "file/printer style/Acrobat." This opens up the printer style-dialogue window. Click on "paper," then "custom" in the drop-down list. Then in the "custom paper size" window, add enough—plenty—to allow not only for bleeds but also printer's marks, if they are needed. You might check with your printer first, however. Sometimes printers like to add their own, and then yours will only get in the way. Another option is to check the "printer's marks" box, but then also check the "crops and bleeds only." Then, only the trims around the page edge and the bleed will show.

Other things to check while you are here include the following.

Click on the "options" tab and make sure that the "download fonts" shows "PostScript and TrueType fonts" rather than "none," which would probably result in all your type defaulting to Courier.

Under "color," you can opt for a composite print, or separations. Check with your printer before selecting the separations option. Usually, printers prefer to generate separations from a composite file.

Under "features," make sure that "printer's default" is selected.

When you return to the "export" window, make sure that in the "printer" section, "Acrobat" is chosen as the style.

None of the other options available under the tabs along the top of this window are particularly important for this setting, so now click on the "edit job options" button.

Under "general," the most important thing is to check that the page range you want to generate is selected.

Next, click on the "compression" tab at the top.

There are three sections, dealing with color images, grayscale images, and monochrome images.

"Downsampling" is how Distiller deals with images of a higher resolution than that required for the preset you have chosen. So, for example, if you have picked "screen," because you are sending the result out as an e-mail attachment, it will want to downsample color and gray images to 72 dpi. Monochrome images are a bit different because they do not have anti-aliased edges, so the dpi needs to be much higher for them to look OK, even on screen. That is why the "screen" preset suggests using 300 dpi.

Distiller will downsize your images to whatever dpi you want. Use 72 dpi for color and grayscale images if you are sending the job as an e-mail attachment, 150 dpi if you are sending it to a digital printer, and at least 300 dpi if it is destined for CTP or offset printing. If you think you need a higher dpi value but are not sure, check the "scanning original material" section (in chapter 13) which discusses the formula involved. At 72 dpi, "average downsampling" is OK. For digital, CTP and offset choose "bicubic downsampling," which uses a method called "weighted averaging" to determine pixel color. It is the slowest method, but the most precise and will give you the smoothest color blends. For monochrome images—line art—you will want 300 dpi for e-mail attachments, 600 dpi for digital printing, and 1200 dpi for CTP or offset.

Leave compression settings on "automatic" for color and gray, "CCITT Group 4" for monochrome. For digital, CTP and offset printing leave quality set to "maximum." (Yes, this will produce a larger file size, but to use anything lower would compromise the quality of the job.) If you are sending a file to be printed, you should always aim for the top in terms of quality. If it is destined to be an e-mail attachment and file size is important then by all means try the different quality settings until you reach an acceptable balance between how big the resulting file is versus how it looks on screen.

Now click on the "fonts" tab.

Check the "embed all fonts" if you are sending the file for printing. Then you do not have to worry. Every font included in the job will be embedded in full. If it is for e-mail, using the "subset embedded fonts" can reduce the size of the result. Type a number in the "%" box, and if you have used less than that percentage of the total characters available, then Distiller will only embed the characters that are actually present.

It is a good idea to select "warn and continue" as the "when embedding fails" option, just in case.

While it is tempting to tell Distiller to never, ever embed fonts like Courier, it can actually help if you do not. Courier is usually the default font when the system cannot find the one it really wants. If it starts showing up, then you know you have a problem—unless you have actually used it in your design, of course.

Now click on the "color" tab.

If you read chapter 10 you will already know something about this area. If you went as far as to create a custom setting for yourself in Photoshop, it should appear in the drop down "settings file" list, and by selecting it you can apply it to your whole file. If not, you can make a variety of other selections including ones that will apply an ICC profile to the whole file or just the images it contains. If you have chosen "screen" as your Distiller preset, all the images in your file will be converted to RGB. If not and you intend to send your file to a printer, you can pick individual working spaces for RGB, CMYK and grayscale images. This is a tricky area—note the inclusion of RGB in the last sentence. What is an option for RGB doing in a setting designated for printing? If you are not sure what to do, do not just pick something—call your printer.

Let us move on to the last tab: "advanced."

This displays a series of on/off options. I suggest leaving them as shown until you are completely sure about what the results of any changes might be.

If you made any changes to the job options, you should now click on "save as" and give your new custom setting a name. If you did not make any changes, click "cancel" to return to the "PDF options" window. Click "export" to apply the selected distiller setting to your file. Acrobat will prompt you for a file name and a location, and then create the PDF document. Open it in Acrobat Reader and check it carefully.

NOTE: If you produced a high-resolution file for CTP or offset printing, running a color proof of it from your desktop system probably will not give great results, because desktop systems are designed to print RGB images and do not usually know what to do with CMYK.

InDesign

InDesign has a "preflight" option enabling you to check fonts, links, graphics, and other information. If you are heading for a print shop, it is a good idea to run this prior to creating a PDF file to ensure that everything meets the necessary specifications.

As with PageMaker, choose "file/export." Immediately you are prompted for a file name and destination. Only then will the "export PDF" window appear. Settings here are very similar to those found in PageMaker, but with some nice additions. Tabs for the different sections are listed down the left-hand side of the export window, and the "style" —the Distiller preset—stays visible in the box at the top. Everything else is much the same until the "marks and bleeds" section, where you can specify the amount of bleed you want to allow for.

In the "advanced" section are several indications of the (current) superiority of InDesign as a page-layout program.

Note that under the style settings for "press" there is no default available for RGB color. That is because there should not be any RGB colors in a job that is destined for print. You can assign an ICC profile here if you assigned one to your document, and a destination profile, too. Again, read chapter 10. If you are still not sure, try to check with someone at the print shop who knows what they are talking about.

If you check the "simulate overprint" box, the PDF file will show you, on screen, the result of any colors you set to overprint others.

Also available here is the ink manager, where you can choose to convert all spot color to process. This is useful if you have been working with a Pantone color but are intending to print only in CMYK.

The "flattener" section deals with how any transparent areas in your work will be dealt with. Basically, if you are using the resulting PDF file for a web site, use "low resolution." For digital printing, use "medium resolution." For CTP or offset printing, use "high resolution."

QuarkXpress

Prior to exporting a file as a PDF, choose "utilities/usage" and check that the fonts showing are the ones you expected and that the images are all linked correctly. If not, the resulting PDF might be in trouble. If a picture is listed as "missing," it means Quark cannot find it in the location from which it was originally linked. You will need to update the connection using the "update" button. If a font appears that you did not expect, click on "show first" to find out where it first appears.

It is not uncommon for Quark files to include line spaces that are specified in a default font such as Arial. Since Arial is a resident font on both PC and Mac systems, there is no need to worry. However, if actual text appears in Arial, and it was supposed to be something else, change it to the correct font and re-save the file before continuing.

As there is no PDF export option in Quark 4, use "file/print" instead. Select Acrobat Distiller as the printer and then click on the "properties" button. There are three tabs here, "layout," "paper/quality," and "Adobe PDF settings." Click on "Adobe PDF settings" first and select the preset you want to use. As with the other page-layout programs, you can edit any of the presets and save it as a custom setting in exactly the same ways as previously described for PageMaker.

Below the "general conversion settings" window are several boxes. If the top one, "do not send fonts to Distiller," is checked, then your type might default to Courier in the result. You may not see this on your system, as the correct font is already installed. But on another system not carrying your particular font, a default will occur. Uncheck the box, and then the fonts you actually want will be embedded. This is a sneaky setting that seems to be able to re-set itself during the night when nobody is watching, so it is important to make sure of it every time you create a PDF file.

I am not aware of any advantages there might be in not sending fonts to Distiller. I have never run into a situation where I would not have wanted the fonts to download, and so I wonder why the setting which chooses to not send the fonts to Distiller seems to be the default.

Under "paper/quality" it should not actually matter which color mode is selected, as the other options you choose in the "print" window should determine this instead. Click on the "advanced" button. Again, it should not be necessary to enter the specific size of paper you are using—but if things do not look right when you eventually check the "preview" tab in the "print" window, return to this area and enter a size which is either the same size as the document page or large enough to accommodate a bleed width.

Under "layout," make sure that the correct orientation is selected. Then click "OK," which will return you to the "print" window.

In the "setup" option make sure that "Acrobat Distiller" is selected as the printer description.

The paper size shown should be either the same as the document page or "custom." For "paper width" you definitely need to enter a large enough measurement to allow for any bleeds in the job. In the lower right corner of the window, again make sure that the orientation shown is correct.

In the "page positioning" window I usually select "centered vertically," but in fact if the other settings you enter are correct it should not end up making any difference.

Now click on the "output" tab. Enter the correct color mode for your job under "print color."

Resolution and "frequency"—which refers to the resolution of the halftone line screen—can usually be overruled by the imagesetter, but it does not hurt to enter "2400" here, just in case. If in doubt, check with your printer. If any RGB colors show up in the list of inks, beware—unless you are generating something for on-screen viewing or a web site, you should go back into the job and either get rid of them or convert to CMYK.

You should not need to change anything under the "options" tab.

Now click on the "document" tab. Do not check "separations" unless your printer has specifically requested them. Whether blank pages are included is entirely up to you, but I think it is always a good idea to include them when sending the file out for print just to avoid confusion among the printers as well as the possibility that a resulting imposition mistake—which could really screw up the whole job—will be blamed on you. If your job has any bleeds, select "centered" from the drop-down list next to "registration" (so that trim marks show up designating the edges of your document page area) and also enter a value of either 1 in or 25 mm for "bleed." Whatever units you are using for the job should show up here automatically. I know that the bleed I just suggested is much more than the $1/8$ in (3 mm) that printers usually request as a bleed amount, but it is better to have too much than too little. So give things a nice wide margin.

Now click on the "preview" tab. The entire page should show up with a highlighted "bleed" area and trim marks clearly visible surrounding the live area of the document page. If not, one of the settings is incorrect and you will have to go back and look for it. If everything looks OK, you are ready to click on the "print" button. Distiller will then prompt you for a name and a location for the PDF file.

Select those, click "save," and you are done. Distiller will do the rest. If you asked it to open the file in Acrobat Reader it will do so immediately after running the job, otherwise you will have to go and find it yourself.

The ability to export (as well as print) a PDF document has been added to Quark versions 5 and 6. The settings given allow you to specify the inclusion of hyperlinks, designate font choices, and change the output resolution and compression methods for images. Otherwise, the output settings are basically the same as for version 4.

Now that everything is ready to roll, there are some things you should know about printers.

Tools of the trade

Most designers do not know that if they ask the printer to take their files, run film and then print the job, then the printer owns the film. Film is technically a "tool of the trade," and actually belongs to the printer unless it is specified on the invoice. Then, and only then, is it yours.

If you tell the printers when you call for an estimate that you want to take the film away with you at the end, they might feel inclined to charge you something extra for doing so. On the other hand, if you do not ask for the film until they call you to say that your job is ready to pick up, you might end up paying for the film twice—once for the set they used to print the job (that belongs to them), and once for the set that you want to take away and keep.

There are two ways to avoid this. One is to get a quote for the job, and after receiving it tell the printer that you want the film specified on the invoice. That is a bit sneaky, however. The best way is to find a "repro house" to output all your film. This is a very good idea, anyway; you get to work with specific people who get used to working with you and the way you like things done. Then you can take the film to any printer you want, and after the job has been run, it is always yours. One thing to note, however, is that repro houses invariably have a preferred proofing method, so make sure you pick one that is right for you and your budget.

Incidentally, while it is sometimes worth making sure that the film is yours to walk away with, this is almost never the case with plates. For one thing, you would have to take them to another shop with exactly the same press. Also, it is easy to damage plates and harder to transport them once they have been on a press, as the edges are crimped from the machine grippers. Because of their sensitivity and odd shape, it is almost certain that by the time you have gone to all the trouble to get them on another press, you will find there is a tiny scratch somewhere that nobody noticed before. And scratches, of course, will show up on the print. If they are in a blank area, they can be dealt with. If they are across a halftone, on the other hand, they are scrap and it has been a big waste of time for everybody—time that most of them will want to charge you for.

Over- and under-runs

Another unpleasant surprise awaits those who need a very specific number of copies of a job printed: if, for example, you have ordered 1,000 copies of a program for the 1,000 people attending an event, but the printers only hand over 900.

Despite what you might think, they are probably under no legal obligation to put the job back on the press. Of course, they will make an adjustment to your bill—but that is also likely to be a shock. It will not be 10% less than the estimate, even though they have come up 10% short on delivery. That is because the job is divided into two areas: "set-up" and "production." Set-up costs are things like film, plates, and setting up machinery such as folders. All this costs the same whether they run one copy or 100,000. Production costs are things like paper, press time, folding time, etc. Obviously, these will vary according to the quantity involved. In this case, you will not get any reduction on the set-up side of things, but you would get a 10% reduction in the production costs.

But you cannot ask the printers to put your job back on the press and print the other 100 copies. Trade conventions in the US and the UK allow as much as a 10% over- or under- run, and the only way to avoid it is to a) read the small print if you are signing a contract, or b) make an agreement beforehand with the printers, in writing, that they supply not less than a specific quantity. In the US, the percentage actually varies from state to state, but tends to be lower than in the UK—for example, in California, it is typically 3%. Of course, in order to guarantee delivery of a fixed number of copies, the printers will probably feel a need to order slightly more paper than they otherwise would, which means they also have to allow for slightly more press time, folding time, binding time, etc. So under these circumstances you should expect to pay a little more.

Cutter draw

There is a nasty little phenomenon that you should know about regarding the trimming of your job because it can affect the quality of the final result even if everything goes well on the press.

It particularly affects cross-overs. These are images which "cross-over" the binding in order to appear on adjacent left- and right-hand pages in a double-page spread. This means each half is printed on a different press sheet. The complete cross-over image only appears when the sheets are collated, folded and trimmed properly.

If cutting is being done prior to the folding (which is most often the case) there is a good chance that you will get some degree of "cutter draw" in the result. This is when the blade of the cutter bends as it cuts through a stack of paper—and the thicker the stack, the greater the effect. At the top of the stack, everything is cut along a straight line. The closer you get to the bottom of the stack, the more the blade has curved and the less accurate the registration will be on all the subsequent operations for those sheets (fig. **17.1**). That can mean that your cross-over does not line up properly across the spine.

In order to avoid this, talk to the printers beforehand and make them aware of your concerns. Ask that the bindery staff be told to cut the job in "small lifts," i.e. a thinner stack of paper as opposed to a thicker one. Again, this will slow things down, so you will be paying a bit more for the job. But remember that old saying: "You can have it quick, cheap or good. Pick any two." Printing is really like that.

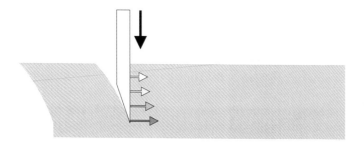

17.1

Seen from the side: the shape of the cutting edge forces the blade into the stack.

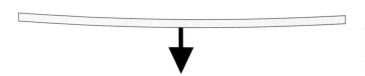

Seen from above: as the blade is anchored at both ends, the result of "cutter draw" is a curved cut.

A final word about printers: when you find some good ones, cherish them. Helpful printers will benefit you and every job you send to them, allowing your clients to recommend you to all their friends with a clear conscience. That is the best kind of publicity you can ever get. I have worked with good printers, and bad, and there is an ocean of difference between them. Most printers will do their absolute best to give you the quality you want, not just because they want you to come back again and again, but because they are decent people who take pride in the job they do.

And a final note about everything else: if this book has helped you, then please use it to help someone else. And I do not mean you have to pass it along to a competitor for free. Just do something for somebody today, and maybe again tomorrow, with this book in mind. Only then will writing it have been worthwhile.

Glossary

Terms that appear in italics are explained elsewhere in the glossary.

algorithm
A mathematically generated pattern that determines the level of complexity in the 8 x 8 *pixel* cells comprising a *JPEG* image.

anti-aliased
When a *bitmap* shape (such as text) is anti-aliased it acquires a slight falling-off of tone around the edges. This enables it to blend in visually with another image much more than would otherwise be possible.

artifacting
When a *JPEG algorithm* is set too low, areas that should appear as flat color in one part of an 8 x 8 *pixel* cell can be distorted by the detail in another.

bit
Image complexity, or depth, is described in terms of bits. A "bit" of information is a single unit of binary information, which can either be "on" or "off." Therefore a "1 bit deep" image is made up of just two colors.

bitmap
Any image which is made up of *pixels* is technically a bitmap, regardless of the actual format. Therefore, *TIFF, JPEG,* and *GIF* images are all bitmaps.

calibration
A method that adjusts highlights, shadows, and mid-tones to determine the overall appearance of an image when printed by a particular method. It can also refer to adjusting the color settings on a monitor so that it produces a more accurate screen image.

clipping path
A *vector* outline that acts as a mask, blocking out any areas of the image which fall outside it.

CMYK
Cyan, magenta, yellow, and black ("key"): the components of the four-color process printing method.

cold-set ink
A *web offset* printing ink, typically used for newsprint, that dries very rapidly. This avoids the need for in-line dryers.

color cast
When a color image has an overall appearance of too much of a particular color it is said to have a "color cast" of that hue.

Compugraphic
Part computer, part machine, the Compugraphic was a popular *phototypesetting* system in the 1970s and 1980s.

computer to plate (CTP)
A printing method that avoids the need for *film* by generating the image directly onto the *plate*.

creep
In book production, a build-up of paper at the binding edge results in each successive set of pages being pushed out by the thickness of the sheet.

Cromalin
A type of high-quality color proof made by fusing extremely thin sheets of *film*, each printed with a toner of the appropriate color, onto a bright white background.

CRT (cathode ray tube)
A cathode ray tube that generates an on-screen image by combining red, green and blue light.

dab test
Testing the accuracy of a *Pantone Matching System* ink mix by spreading a very small amount of it onto a sheet of paper. This is typically done right beside the press with the printer's finger.

DCS2 (desktop color separation 2)
A very useful multi-channel file format that allows *spot* colors such as Pantone mixes to be added to *CMYK* images.

densitometer
A hand-held device that measures the density of the ink on a printed sheet.

direct imaging (DI)
A printing method that avoids not only *film* but *plates*, too. DI electrostatically generates the image on a revolving drum in much the same way as a laser printer. Therefore, each successive page can be different.

dither
Scattering *pixels* of one color across pixels of another creates the visual appearance of a third color which is not actually present. This enables *GIF* images, which can hold a maximum of 256 colors, to appear to be much more complex.

dot gain
When a *halftone* image is physically (rather than digitally) transferred from one medium to another, the dots tend to change size. Technically, the change undergone by the 50% dot is called "dot gain," although the term has come to refer more to changes across the entire tonal range.

dpi
Dots per inch, the dots actually being square *pixels*. This is the accepted measurement defining the resolution of an image made up of pixels.

EPS (encapsulated PostScript)
An image format capable of holding both *vector* and *bitmap* information.

film
A transparent acetate sheet coated with an opaque photosensitive emulsion on one side.

flexography
A printing method capable of printing on non-absorbent surfaces that uses a molded rubber sheet as a *plate*.

folding dummy
A folded sample of an intended print job that is typically sent to the printer as part of the designer's proof so that possible misunderstandings in folding, cutting, and scoring can be avoided.

frequency-modulated screen (see **stochastic screen**)

galley
Phototypesetting machines of the 1970s and 1980s imaged their text onto long rolls of photographic paper or *film*. These were known as galleys of type.

GIF (graphics interchange format)
An image made up of a restricted (*indexed*) palette of 256 colors, one of which can be designated as transparent. This makes *GIF* images ideal for websites where they can be used for irregular shapes such as logos which can then be "floated" over colored backgrounds. GIF images are not suitable for inclusion in a job destined for *offset* printing.

glyph
A specific form of character such as a *swash* or small cap alternative to the regular form.

grain direction
The fibers from which paper is made tend to line up together during the manufacturing process. This is then known as the grain direction of the sheet. Paper folds more easily and cleanly with the grain than against it.

gravure
A printing method using etched cells in a rigid *plate* to hold more, or less, of the ink which then results in a correspondingly darker or lighter printed area.

grayscale
An image made up of 256 shades of gray pixels which is then printed using black ink.

gripper edge
The edge of a press sheet that is grabbed by a series of mechanical "grippers" in order to pull it through the press.

halftone
An image that has been converted into a vertical and horizontal grid of dots of different sizes.

HTML (hypertext markup language)
One of the main codes used for website layouts.

image header
Because it is not possible to see an actual *EPS* file when placed into a page layout, an image header (a low-resolution *TIFF* image) appears instead, showing the position and content of the EPS image.

imagesetter
A machine that digitally images *film* and/or *plates*.

imposition
The layout governing how pages in a multi-page job need to be arranged so that they end up in the correct order.

indexed color
The color mode of *GIF* images, which can hold a maximum of 256 colors.

interpolation
Mathematically rather than optically increasing the resolution of an image.

Iris proof
A form of high-quality proof generated by a *PostScript* inkjet printer.

JPEG or **JPG (joint photographic experts group)**
An image format supporting *grayscale*, *RGB* and *CMYK* color but which uses a *lossy* compression method. However, at high-quality levels, the loss is almost impossible to detect, while the file size is much smaller than the same image saved as a *TIFF*. Nevertheless, JPEGs should not be included in a job destined for *offset* printing.

LAB mode
A wide-gamut file format made up of three channels: "lightness," "A," and "B."

laser proof
When a job is sent to a print shop, it is usually accompanied by a full, laser-printed copy intended to show where everything is supposed to be on the final print. Its accuracy in terms of color varies a great deal and should usually only be considered as an approximation of the final print.

letterpress
A printing method relying on the assembly of metal type characters and etched images into a matrix which can then be inked.

ligature
A single typographical character that combines two or more other characters.

Linotype
Part computer, part machine, the Linotype was a popular *phototypesetting* system in the 1970s and 1980s.

lossless
An image-compression method that does not result in any data or quality loss.

lossy
An image compression system that results in a degree of data, and therefore quality, loss.

lpi (lines per inch)
The standard measurement of *halftone* resolution. It refers to the number of rows of halftone dots there are per inch.

Matchprint
Similar to a *Cromalin*, a Matchprint is a type of high-quality color proof made by fusing extremely thin sheets of *film*, each printed with a toner of the appropriate color, onto a bright white background.

moiré pattern
An interference pattern caused by the dot grids ("screens") of two or more colors in an image being set at incorrect angles. This causes the dots to collide unevenly.

Newton's Rings
Pressure points against the glass of a vacuum platemaker caused by small foreign objects trapped inside. These appear as concentric rings of dark colors.

nodes
Anchor points that determine the shape of a *vector* path.

offset litho
A printing method in which the image on a *plate* is transferred ("offset") to an intermediate roller prior to final transfer to the paper.

optimization
Cutting down on image file size while trying to maintain the quality of its appearance.

Pantone Inc.
The Pantone Corporation produces many aids to designers and printers such as the Pantone Process Guide (for selecting *CMYK* tints) and the *Pantone Matching System* which allows a wide range of non-CMYK colors to be accurately mixed by formula.

Pantone Matching System
A range of printing ink colors that can be easily mixed by formula from a set of base colors.

PDF (portable document format)
A form of *PostScript* developed by Adobe that enables a printable document to be generated as anything from a low-resolution screen image to a high-resolution file suitable for *offset* printing.

perfecting
A printing process that applies the image to both sides of the sheet during the same run through the press.

phototypesetting
Generating text using photographic means, typically using a hybrid machine (such as *Compugraphic*) which is part mechanical and part digital.

picking
This occurs when the ink is unable to stick to the paper and peels back off onto the rollers of the printing press instead.

pixel
The building blocks of digital images, pixels are small squares of color. The resolution of an image is determined by how many pixels there are per linear inch. The color range of the pixels is determined by the *bit* depth of the image.

plate
A sheet of, typically, aluminium or zinc coated with a photosensitive emulsion. When developed, either the remaining emulsion or the exposed background attracts ink.

posterize
Restricting an image so that it displays only a specific number of colors.

PostScript
A digital encoding language developed by Adobe.

PostScripting
Generating a digital file in a *PostScript* format, usually in order to overcome problems that can arise when transferring a document from a PC computer to a Mac *imagesetter*.

rasterize
This is the method by which a *bitmap* made up of *pixels* (which are square and have no space between them) is turned into a *halftone* made up of round dots arranged on a horizontal and vertical grid.

registration

When a multi-color image is printed, it is essential that each color is laid down in exactly the right place. If not, the result is said to be "out of register."

RGB

A color space comprising combinations of red, green, and blue light.

saddle-stitching

A binding method using metal staples for publications such as magazines which usually contain 64 pages or less.

screen density

The number of *halftone* dots to a linear inch determines the screen density of an image.

screenprinting

Printing by forcing ink through a membrane stretched over a frame, on which the image acts as a stencil.

set-off

The unwanted transfer of part of a printed image from one sheet to another. This usually occurs within a stack of freshly printed sheets due to a lack of *offset* spray, or from too much ink, or both.

sheet-fed press

A printing press that uses sheets of paper rather than a continuous roll.

sheetwise format

A print run in which a different set of *plates* is used to print each side of the sheet.

signature

A multi-page section of a book which is printed as a single, larger sheet. This can then be folded and collated with any other signatures prior to binding and a final trim.

spot color or **special color**

A specific non-*CMYK* ink color.

stochastic screen or **frequency-modulated screen**

An image generated using an apparently random spray of extremely small dots of color and which is therefore incapable of generating a *moiré pattern*, regardless of the number of colors involved.

swashes

Alternative character choices within a given typeface such as more ornate capitals.

TIFF or **TIF (targa image file format)**

An uncompressed *bitmap* format that supports a variety of color modes including *grayscale*, *RGB,* and *CMYK*.

tint jump

A sudden jump in tint density caused by a meeting of the individual dots comprising the *halftone* screen.

trapping

The enlargment of a light-colored area so that it slightly overlaps into an adjacent darker color, thereby compensating for slight imperfections of *registration* on the press which might otherwise cause a gap between the two.

vector

A mathematically defined outline to which color and thickness can be assigned. This is the native object format for elements drawn using Adobe Illustrator, CorelDraw, and Macromedia Freehand.

web offset litho
A printing method in which the image is transferred from the *plate* to an intermediate roller prior to being transferred to the paper, and which prints on a continuous roll rather than sheets.

work-and-tumble format
A print run in which the paper is printed on one side, then turned long edge over long edge before being run through the press again.

work-and-turn format
A print run in which the paper is printed on one side, then turned short edge over short edge before being run through the press a second time.

Index

Page numbers in *italics*
refer to illustrations